Can't Meditate
Won't Meditate

Mindfulness in Odd Moments

by

Sue Breton

Author's Note

There are audio downloads which accompany this book for which an internet connection is needed.

For those who are unable to access or use these I have included written instructions for doing the meditations at the back of this book. Please be aware, however, that the audio method is preferable.

Published by Anxaid

Coleford, Glos, UK

www.anxaid.com

Publisher's Note: All examples contained in this book are the experiences of real people but the names, sometimes the gender, and other details have been changed in order to protect anonymity.

This book is written in UK English.

Can't Meditate, Won't Meditate/Sue Breton

ISBN-10: 1500741779
ISBN-13: 978-1500741778

Dedication

This book is dedicated to all those who believed in me enough to join in with my mindfulness courses and trusted me despite being asked to do things which might have seemed a bit crackpot at first. Thank you for your support, for the fun we had along the way and for helping me prove this was possible.

Table of Contents

Dedication 5

Introduction 11

What Is the Aim of This Book? 14

1 - Why Do I Need Mindfulness? 17

Are You the Person You Truly Want To Be? 17

How do I know what I'm going to tell you will work? 18

The Calm Reservoir 20

Do You Have Negative Focus Habits? 25

Do You Really Want It Enough? 26

So What Do You Have To Do? 29

2 - Why Is Change So Hard? 33

Why Do We Expect Everything To Be Easy? 35

Nobody Can Do It for You 38

3 – Do You Know What the Biggest Hurdle Is? 39

What Is Being in the Moment? 43

Test Yourself 52

4 – How to Develop Your Awareness 53

As If for the First Time 54

In the Moment 60

Test Yourself 63

5 - Learn To Meditate on Touch 65

After Brief Touch 68

The Monkey and Banana 70

Action Points..72

6 – Does Your Alarm System Need a Service?...........73

Action Points..86

Test Yourself..87

7 – How To Meditate on Sound...................................89

8 - Stop the Negative Past Colouring Now..................95

Changes can be stressful..107

Why laid-back people don't often get anxious................111

The Tiger and the Stawberry..113

Action Points..116

Test Yourself..117

9 - What To Do When You Can't Do Anything...........119

What Can We Control?..121

Resistance..125

The Two Monks and the Beautiful Girl............................136

Action Points..138

Test Yourself..139

10 - Meditating on Your Breath.................................141

11 - Do We Always Need To Have an Opinion?.........145

The Abuse of Language...151

When is judgment justified?...153

Working harder and harder...157

Action Points..158

Test Yourself..159

12 - What If You've Got It and You Don't Want It?..................161

The Stonecutter 169

Action Point 172

13 - Twinges Meditation 173

14 - If You Don't Want It, Why Think About It? 177

I Don't Believe It! 189

Action Point 191

15 - A Dirty Word You May Not Know 193

Should 193

Feeling Guilty 197

It's Not Always About You 198

Do We Need To Worry What Others Think? 201

Getting in Touch with Now 203

It Will Pass 205

Test Yourself 206

16 - The Big 'T' 207

Phobias and Mindfulness 215

The Boastful Archer 221

Action Point 222

17 - What To Do with Thoughts When You Meditate 223

18 - Where To Now? 231

Whatever Comes, Whatever Goes Meditation 233

Final Words 234

Answers to Test Yourself Questions 237

End Note 241

Other Books by Sue Breton 242

Link to Meditation Downloads 243

Meditation Instructions 243

Introduction

You may have heard of mindfulness. Suddenly it is gaining momentum and is finding it's way into all walks of life. There are mindfulness courses run by mental health services, mindfulness courses in the workplace, mindfulness teaching in schools and so on.

Mindfulness wasn't recently invented. It has been part of Buddhism for over a thousand years. It is only recently that the West has caught on to its benefits. You don't, however, have to be a Buddhist to practise it in a form that is useful in everyday life.

There is good research evidence that being more mindful in our lives enables us to feel calmer generally and feel more in control of what we are able to control. It has also been shown to reduce episodes of depression in those who were prone to having them. So what are you waiting for . . . ?

Learning mindfulness sounds wonderful . . . until you try to do it.

My guess is that you are reading this book because you did like the sound of mindfulness, but then you tried it and found out that it involved MEDITATION! And you just couldn't do it, so you gave up.

Perhaps you never even started because you thought the whole idea of meditation was a bit too new-age for you as it conjured up images of joss sticks and sitting cross-legged on the floor?

Or maybe you knew from the start that you wouldn't be able to do it so rather than wasting everyone's time you never tried. But did you then feel cheated as if you were missing out on the party?

Many people start a mindfulness course but then they find their minds wandering during the meditations. They conclude they must be doing it wrong because they can't maintain concentration.

The good news here is that none of us can!

The sort of concentration most beginners expect to be able to achieve would only come with years of serious practice. And for meditation to be effective to a useful degree you don't have to be that good at it.

I'm here to tell you that meditation doesn't have to involve sitting on the floor, burning incense, chanting, or even doing anything that would draw attention to you in a public place. You can meditate on the bus if you want to and nobody else need be any the wiser!

What Is the Aim of This Book?

There are two parts to mindfulness—the theory and the practice. Some people are drawn to one and not the other, some recognise the value of both.

I have assumed that you are reading this book because you like the idea of mindfulness but just can't seem to get into it. This is probably because you are a very logical person who needs to understand reasons and make sense of things for them to be meaningful. There's nothing wrong with that! People also vary in their preferred learning styles. Life would be dull if we were all the same.

I have therefore concentrated mainly on the reasons why learning mindfulness is helpful. I have included some brief meditation exercises as these are essential. For those who, by the end of the book, feel a need to indulge in longer and more advanced meditation sessions, there is a huge amount of material of this kind available elsewhere. My aim is to get people over the initial hurdle.

For the logical thinkers to whom this may appeal, I have included a few questions at the end of some chapters so you can test out your knowledge as we go. Naturally you only have to do these if you want to.

So if you are now prepared to keep an open mind and allow yourself to believe that it is possible to learn to be more mindful in your everyday life without struggle and without feeling stupid, then read on.

1 – Why Do I Need Mindfulness?

Are You the Person You Truly Want To Be?

Do you have something in your life which is preventing you from being the person you want to be or from living the life you want to live?

Have you had bad experiences in your past which won't seem to let you move forward?

Are you maybe shy or lacking in confidence?

Do you feel as if others push you around yet you seem unable to stand up for yourself?

Do you tend to feel down a lot of the time?

Do you have a problem which you've battled with for what seems ages but got nowhere?

ACTION POINT:

Can you easily fill in the blanks in any of the following sentences?
(Pause and think what you'd put before continuing)
If only I had/didn't have/could/hadn't ... then I'd ...

If only I hadn't ... then I'd ...

If only I could ... then I'd ...

If only ... hadn't happened then I'd ...

Or do you just not look forward to each new day? Then this is the book for you!

How do I know what I'm going to tell you will work?

I know you're sceptical because it may sound too good to be true. If it's that easy, why hasn't someone told you about it before? If it's that simple, why isn't everyone happy? In many cases it's because they don't know how. Let me explain how I came to be writing this.

I'm a clinical psychologist, working in the NHS, but over thirty years ago I had a brief period in my own life when my own anxieties got the better of me and I was housebound for a few weeks, too afraid to go out.

I took what had happened to me as a challenge. As a psychologist I was fully aware of what was going on but just not sure what to do about it. I knew that nobody could cure me but me. So I set about planning how I might go about changing things and putting it into practice. I analysed what I did, what worked and what didn't.

I realise that many people who have anxiety problems are very afraid of what's happening to them. I accept that I started from a better place because at least my knowledge allowed me to understand. But I still had to use what I knew to overcome it.

That experience is now available to you, right here. I know it works because I did it. There were times when I started to think that various things I was trying weren't working. When I re-analysed these I always found that it was because I wasn't actually doing what I should have been.

My original theories as to what should work did pan out. What I thought would work, did work, and still does. So how did I go about it?

The Calm Reservoir

I suspected that keeping my arousal level low was the key. Arousal level? Yes, that feeling that comes and goes depending what's going on.

Arousal levels go up when we don't know what's coming. Or when we do know what's coming and we aren't looking forward to it. If you have to go to the dentist later today you may notice your arousal level go up a bit each time the thought enters your head. How far it goes up depends on how much you dislike going to the dentist.

It may also go up if you see a brown envelope on the doormat and you know you have no money to pay bills. It will go up if you start worrying about something.

These are all examples of the arousal going up with negative feelings. Of course, it also goes up when we have positive feelings. For example, if you are watching the lottery draw and your first number comes up . . . it goes up a bit. If your second number comes up . . . it goes up a bit further . . . by the time your last number and all the others in between have come up as well it may even be off the scale!

But it is not the positive arousal that causes us problems. The one to watch out for is the negative arousal—those feelings of dread.

For instance I'd noticed that whenever I had a thought which contained any degree of anxiety and my arousal level began to rise, I'd start to feel uneasy. I noticed that if I then moved my thoughts to the present moment and made my muscles relax, I could keep feeling sort of ok for the time being.

I worked at it. I noticed that each time I thought about anything which I couldn't see or touch at that moment, the arousal level would creep up. This was because nearly every time my thoughts wandered from the present they had gone to find a worry of some kind!

I would have a sudden thought such as, "What if I don't feel well enough to make the kids' tea?" To think such a thing now is laughable, but at that time it was scary. When you are in a state of hyper-arousal most of the time the silliest little things take on huge significance.

So I used to imagine I had a huge reservoir of calm inside me. This was filled with lovely blue water. The higher I could keep the level in the reservoir, the more it would take to make me over-anxious. If, on the other hand, I allowed the level to drop then I could expect to become anxious at the slightest provocation.

The water would start to seep out of the reservoir each time I allowed myself to focus on any negative thought or emotion. My head's thinking habits, like everyone's, would constantly interrupt and invade my head with thoughts of all manner of trivia that weren't actually present in the here and now. At this stage many of them began with the dreaded, "What if . . . ?"

Each time that happened I would say to myself, "At this moment and in this place I'm safe." Then I'd focus my attention on doing something such as ironing a garment, dusting, doing a row of knitting, etc.

I found that I didn't have to concentrate in any depth on any of these activities for any length of time. I just had to allow myself to be aware of doing the activity. (You will understand better exactly what this means when we come to the meditations later).

Over time the technique worked. As the days and weeks passed the level in my reservoir rose higher and higher. Bit by bit the anxieties went away, and they stayed away. That all happened thirty years ago and I have never been back there since.

This was all before Jon Kabat Zinn introduced the concept of Mindfulness to health settings. But I later realised that what I had instinctively used was a simple form of mindfulness.

In recent years, I have taught mindfulness as a tool with which people can help themselves. I have developed a programme which is easy to do as part of everyday life. This programme will help you to realise how the thinking habits, which you learnt as you grew up, are getting in the way of the life you want.

Do You Have Negative Focus Habits?

Our society tends to focus on what's wrong rather than on what's right. At school we often had the faults in our homework underlined and the good bits passed over. Many parents ignore their children when the children are being good, but tell them off i.e. pay attention to them, when they're naughty.

Is it any wonder then that most of us grow up constantly judging ourselves for our failures and when we haven't got it 'right'? We never focus on our good qualities but are always trying to correct what we think is 'wrong' with us.

How often do you make New Year's Resolutions which are aimed at making you a 'better' person in some way? And because you keep reminding yourself about ways in which you need to do better, by definition you are also giving yourself the message that you aren't good enough the way you are.

This constant focus on the negatives rather than the positives is at the root of much unhappiness, anxiety and depression. The programme I have been teaching for the past ten years allows you to accept yourself the way you are and focus instead of what's good in your life. Those who have completed it have found their lives have changed as a result. This is often not because anything appears to have changed on the outside, but because what goes on inside most certainly has—and for the better.

My aim is to make you aware of what it is that is keeping you where you are and then show you how to break free from it.

Do You Really Want It Enough?

My skills were honed while working in the UK for the National Health Service. One disadvantage of free healthcare is that those using it don't always value what they are getting.

In my job I saw numerous individuals who turned up saying they wanted help but then proving totally unwilling to actually put any of the guidance into practice. They would come up with all manner of excuses for this, the classic being, "I didn't have time," or, "I forgot."

(I also saw many more who were prepared to give it a go and to whom this book is dedicated).

I'm not offering a quick fix here. It does work—every time—but you have to actually follow the instructions and do what it says. You have to keep at it. I have done my best to make it as appealing as it can be.

There are available numerous books and CDs designed to teach mindfulness. Most of them, however, are too complex for the average newcomer for whom the idea of just meditating for minutes at a time holds no real attraction. The challenge for me was to devise a way of presenting the material so as to make it attractive to two groups in particular.

The first group was those living very busy lives who wanted to do it but would not readily devote a great deal of time to it.

For them I had to develop something that was simple to incorporate into everyday life without having to set aside special time to do it. In order to help people remember, I incorporated the exercises into normal everyday activities so you don't have to put yourself out unduly to do them. Once you get the habit of doing them as part of your daily life, they then become your new habits. The more you do them, the easier it is to do them.

The second group was those who wanted to give it a go but felt unable to stay in a room with others or started, "what if . . .?" thinking the instant we started a meditation and began to feel panicky. This group also included those who felt unable to concentrate on meditations. For this group in particular, the longer, focused meditations taught elsewhere as part of mindfulness, would not be easy and people would give up.

I have found that once people understand something about mindfulness and the practice of it by following this programme, they are then able to move on to some of the more detailed material available elsewhere if they wish to know more.

So I introduced very short and simple meditations with lots of guidance. These don't allow the more anxious participants and those with wandering minds to drift off into their own worlds, at least, not for too long.

So What Do You Have To Do?

Apart from reading the book, you don't have to set aside large chunks of time each day to practise meditating or anything like that. You will need to listen to the free downloadable meditation tracks at least once to understand how to do the meditations. But you don't have to play them afterwards in order to practise unless you choose to. You don't need to find extra time. The meditations can be done anywhere at any time as long as you're awake.

Now that really does sound too good to be true, doesn't it?

As for those who claim, "It's hard" or "It's not as easy as that!" I say this... Look back at what you answered to the questions on page 18. What did you put was holding you back from having the life you wanted?

Imagine you are dangling from a tenth floor balcony by a ten foot rope. How you came to be there is irrelevant because you are there and you have to deal with it. There's nobody else around to help and nobody is likely to come to your aid.

You have two choices, you either summon all your

strength and effort to haul yourself back up the rope to safety, or you don't. The result of doing nothing will be eventually that you will tire and fall. The first option requires effort but you get your life back. But it has to be your choice.

I know that somebody will be saying that the situation is different because it's life or death. We all seem to find reserves of determination when the chips are really down. So, in that case, are you saying that you are not really committed to changing your life for the better and getting free of what's holding you back?

If that's the case be honest with yourself and give up now because with that attitude you'll get nowhere.

This brings me to a very old joke, but one which is very relevant here...

How many psychologists does it take to change a light bulb?

Answer: One, but it must really want to change.

And that is what lies at the root of success—you have to want it.

This programme requires no extra physical effort and no long practice sessions (unless you want to have them). But it does require motivation and the real desire to change.

To return to the start of this chapter—why do you need mindfulness? The answer is that you don't. Nobody needs it. People can exist fine without ever having it. Ask instead, what will learning mindfulness do for me? The answer to that is as much as you allow it to.

At the end of the NHS courses I've run we've handed out a questionnaire. It is entirely optional whether this is completed or not and participants only have to answer those questions which they choose to answer. One response which repeatedly appears is along the lines of: "I wish I'd known about this years ago. It's so obvious but you'd never do it unless you were taught to!"

The choice is yours.

2 – Why Is Change So Hard?

Who hasn't at some time in their life tried to change a habit? It may be going on a diet, giving up smoking, getting up earlier, studying a language, etc. Presumably most of us start out on this path because we want to change and we believe that the change is good for us in some way.

But in order to get this new benefit we usually have to change something we do now. Maybe we have to give up something we're comfortable with and which we do without any effort at all, automatically even.

For example, the diet may go ok to begin with but the weight doesn't come off fast enough to be a reward in itself. One or two days on the diet won't get us into the size smaller jeans we crave. The fact that the bar of chocolate is here and now, whereas the smaller jeans are still pie in the sky, means no contest—the chocolate wins.

The Italian lessons are fun at the start and we feel good at being able to say, "How are you?" in another language. But after a few lessons we realise that it is going to take a very long time and much effort before we can hold a conversation in Italian or watch a film without subtitles. The enthusiasm starts to wane. Instead of going to the classes or doing the homework, which requires a bit of effort, we take the easy effortless option and spend the time watching TV or doing something which gives immediate pleasure.

On the courses I've run, whenever I reach the point of describing what it will take for change to occur there will always be someone who will say, "But it's not as easy as that!" or words to that effect.

Why Do We Expect Everything To Be Easy?

There's something of a paradox here if you think about it. On the one hand we tend to be suspicious of something for nothing. We have a belief in our culture which tells us, "no pain, no gain." But then when we want something that requires a small amount of effort and sacrifice (pain) we tend to give up, or make excuses to let ourselves off the hook.

Generally speaking, when you have a physical ailment of some kind and are referred to a specialist, you expect that specialist to have the answer. Not only that, but you also expect them to either do something to you such as an operation to fix something , or give you pills that will sort it out. You expect to be passive, not to have to do anything much for yourself.

When you call the plumber to fix the washing machine, you expect him to get on with it and just let you know when it's done.

But changing ourselves is different. You've probably tried to do this with some aspect of yourself before—and failed. Now you might be asking, "If it's really going to give me a better life, why don't I keep doing it anyway?"

Because it means changing one of the hardest things of all—habit.

Changing the habits of a lifetime needs to be done at a slow and steady pace. Changes need to be gradually added into everyday behaviours so they eventually become the new habits. As we all know, once we have learnt a habit it's hard to lose it again! Therefore slow and steady = permanent.

Change is scary, even when it's good. It doesn't happen overnight so some degree of ongoing encouragement is usually necessary. If left to our own devices it is easy to drift back into old habits.

Brains like predictability and sameness. If they've come across something before they know how it will turn out. Brains like to know the score. They don't like the new and different because they don't know what to expect and it could prove dangerous.

So we all find we are directed towards the known behaviours and responses even when these may be not what we really want. If we try and change too much about our everyday routines too fast we will start to feel a bit uneasy even when it's something for the better.

So for change to be successful it needs to be taken slowly so as to be almost invisible (I said 'almost' not totally!). It needs to be so easy to implement as part of everyday life that you don't have to make any great effort to do it.

So I designed the programme to be just that— different enough to be interesting yet ordinary enough to feel effortless. The steps required are small and are things you can do as part of your normal everyday life. If you keep taking small steps you will reach the goal. Once the programme has become a normal part of your everyday life you just keep doing it.

Nobody Can Do It for You

When it comes to changing you, the work must be done by you. There is no magic wand. The only thing that can control your thoughts is you. Therefore, unless you start to use that power for your own good, nothing will change. My task is to teach you how to go about it.

So when someone says, "But that's hard," I point out that it isn't hard in the sense of being difficult, because anyone can do it, if they choose to.

It's not hard in the sense of requiring huge physical effort, like running a marathon. You don't have to physically do anything you don't normally do.

It's not hard, but it requires persistence. You have to keep at it to get results and you have to remember to do it.

But you don't have to sacrifice something you enjoy in order to do it. If anything, the biggest danger is from the fact that the steps are so small and simple. It's easy to not bother to do them. That would be the biggest mistake.

3 – Do You Know What the Biggest Hurdle Is?

Thinking habits!

At this moment, as you read this book, it is extremely unlikely that you are in any real physical danger. Anyone whose life was truly at risk wouldn't be reading. Anyone in real danger at this very moment would not be analysing how they felt. They'd be totally focused on the danger and what was happening to them and what they could do to escape or avoid it.

You, on the other hand, are probably sitting safely at home, or on a train, or at your desk, or maybe even lying tucked up in your bed. Therefore, any anxiety or other negative feeling you may have just now is coming into your awareness through your thoughts. You're worried, anxious or down because of what you're thinking about and not because of what is actually happening to you in the here and now.

This thinking habit demands closer attention

Are you aware how much time you spend thinking? Probably not. Most of the thinking we do, we do in words. Even when we think in pictures we usually then comment to ourselves in words about those pictures. We have silent discussions and arguments with ourselves, in our heads. I call these 'head conversations'.

Our use of words means we are able to imagine all kinds of things which are not actually happening here and now. How many of the following can you catch yourself having a head conversation about today?

1. Events in the past which have caused you pain or distress of some kind.

2. Things which you now feel guilty about.

3. Things which may happen in the future which could scare you.

4. Things which are expected of you which you feel you can't live up to, etc.

You get the idea . . .

Whatever it was, if it's something in the past we then re-live all that hurt and anguish by thinking about it all again in the present moment.

If it's something that hasn't happened yet, is worrying about it now going to change whatever it will be in any way for the better?

The feelings we have now, as we think, are due to something which happened in the past or which might happen in the future. We are not living in the present moment at all . . .

***

ACTION POINT:

Stop reading for a moment and close your eyes. Now spend the next two minutes not thinking . . .

***

I'm willing to bet that during that exercise you either drifted off and started planning for later by thinking about what you had to do next. If not you started wondering what was the point of what you were doing, etc.

Maybe you even thought that not thinking for two minutes was a stupid idea so you didn't bother. If you did, even coming to that conclusion involved thinking.

Whatever your response was I'll bet that you did think something. I'll bet too that you then maybe tried to get rid of the thoughts so you could do what I had asked and not think.

Thinking in this way is a habit we develop as we go through life. In many cases, the older we are and the less we have to do, the more we think.

People who suffer with depression tend to lose the enthusiasm for doing anything at all. Bit by bit they spend more and more time just thinking and not about happy things either. The worse our problems become, the more we tend to think about them, and worry about them.

What Is Being in the Moment?

A key concept of mindfulness is that of being 'in the moment'. Living in the present moment means keeping your mind and your body together in the here and now. You may be having thoughts, but you are not engaging with them.

Being in the moment is to just be aware of where you are and what you are doing and experiencing but not having to put any of it into thoughts. But if you are reading this book I doubt you are able to do this . . . yet.

Apart from people who have learnt the techniques of mindfulness, being present in the moment is largely the domain of very young children and animals.

Watch a toddler who hasn't yet learnt to talk. Whatever that child does, it is totally engrossed in it. As the child attempts to build a tower of bricks, its focus is on the feel of the toy and the action it is taking. It plays with a ball unaware of anything else.

The child is not at the same time wondering what it will have for tea, or where its mother is. Should the child become aware that its mother is not nearby, it will

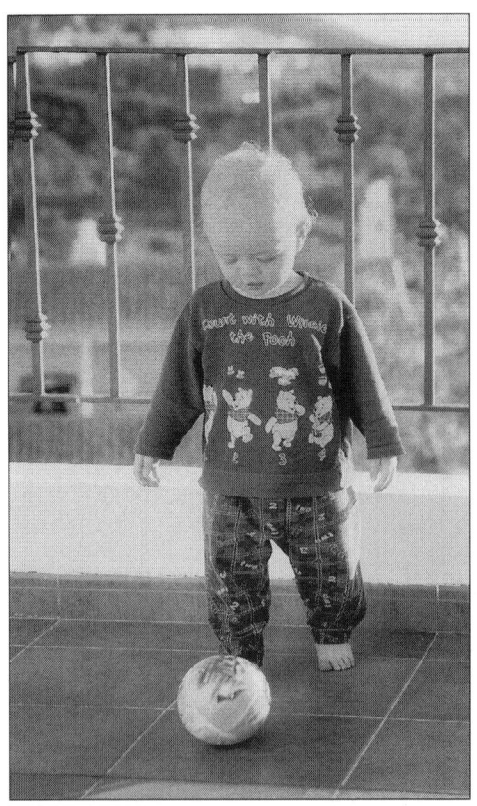

totally abandon the bricks and attempt to find her. It will then keep searching or calling or crying until someone or something else captures its attention.

Your dog or cat wanders around and does whatever it wants at that moment.

Imagine you let the dog out into the garden and then became engrossed in a film on TV? Perhaps several hours pass before you hear the dog whining.

When you finally open the door, the dog doesn't waste time reproaching you and telling you off for forgetting it. Most probably it will shake itself and then go and find a nice warm spot in front of the fire to fall asleep. What matters to the dog is now. Being shut in the garden is already a past event. The dog has moved on.

On a daily basis neither the small child nor the pet is thinking about bad things that have happened in the past. Dogs don't commit suicide. They may get run over, but when they do, it's not because that was their intention.

Without language to help with the thoughts, it is very difficult to consider how much better or worse things might be. Small children and pets are aware of what they can feel, hear, taste, smell, but are not thinking about things which they can't feel, hear, taste or smell at that moment. Neither do they keep up a running commentary in their heads as to how well, or not, they might be doing whatever it is. They simply do it.

As for the rest of us we spend far too much of our time doing commenting. We are there in our lives physically, yet only truly experiencing it through the comments we are making in our heads. It's as if we're TV sports reporters telling ourselves what's going on and why, yet not actually experiencing it for real.

Although we all seem to recognize that it's our thoughts which cause us the grief, we seem powerless to do anything about them. In order to make this point with patients I often start by saying, "Imagine you had a switch on the side of your head so you could switch your brain off . . ." I rarely need to go any further as, almost without exception, they instantly know exactly what that would mean for them and smile at the very idea.

Pets and small children are easily distracted simply because whatever they focus on at any time, they do 100%. Therefore if you can lure their focus onto something else, the whole of their awareness goes too.

No doubt we've all at some time tried to comfort a baby whose mother has had to leave it for a time. When the baby notices she's gone it becomes distressed. In order to calm it we do all we can to focus its attention on something else. We dangle things in front of it, we may attempt to sing to it, we jiggle it about . . . Once we have engaged its attention it stops fretting about its mother and then generally appears to 'forget' her existence until she reappears, or something causes it distress.

On the other hand, have you ever tried to take an older child's or an adult's mind off something which is distressing them? It's much more difficult because part of their focus will try to remain on what's troubling them. And how do they maintain this focus? By thinking in words about it.

We tend to constantly think about what we have done or what we've yet to do. We rarely live in the now moment. So if we are using our thoughts to bring this grief into our present moment, we could conclude that it's our thinking habits which cause us problems rather than what actually happens to us.

Many people seek therapy because distressing things have happened to them in the past. They tend to assume that in order to get past these they need to be talked about. Although this is true of some things, it is by no means necessary in all, or even most, cases.

I know there will be protests about that statement. People will be saying that they must think about problems and things which worry them. Whether that is the case we will consider in a later chapter. For now I just want you to agree that such thinking actually makes you feel bad regardless of whether you consider you should do it or not.

***

ACTION POINT:

Take a moment now and observe yourself and your situation. Look around. At this instant you are safe, reasonably comfortable, just reading a book. Don't think about anything in the past or the future . . . Just for now pretend you have the mind of a newborn baby. You don't yet have the power of speech, so you can't think in words. You can only directly experience the sensations being picked up by your five senses i.e. what you can see, feel, hear, touch or taste. You have no understanding of either yesterday or tomorrow. Life is only now, in this moment.

***

Do this for a minute or so before reading on . . . How did that experience differ from the one we did a few moments ago?

Were you able to do that? Or did you start wondering why you were doing it as you did it? Did you perhaps skip that exercise and continue reading? Did you decide it was stupid to do that? Did you catch yourself thinking about what you were doing, putting words to describe what your senses were picking up? if you skipped it, why did you decide to skip it? Be honest with yourself.

The main problem for most of us is not only that we think too much, but that we then react to those same thoughts as if they are someone in authority telling us to do something important! We all have too many 'head conversations'.

If, when asked to do the exercise just now, you started asking yourself why you were doing it, or you decided it was silly and chose not to bother, you were having 'head conversations'. These are silent discussions you have with yourself.

I simply asked you to allow yourself, in the relative safety of wherever you are reading this, to pretend you were unable to use language, and to just experience the input of your senses, as if you were a baby again. But you couldn't just do that.

Did you question what you were being asked to do? Did you perhaps pass some judgment on the purpose of the exercise, or on how well you managed to do it? Was any of this relevant to the requirements of the exercise? No, but you did it anyway.

To become more mindful you first have to become more aware of just how many of these 'head conversations' you have. As with many bad habits, we cannot change them until we become fully aware of when we are lapsing into them.

Therefore many of the little exercises included here are aimed at just helping you to gently develop this awareness. What you then choose to do about it will be up to you, although I will offer suggestions.

Just reading this book may indeed develop your self-awareness, but that alone won't bring about any lasting change. In order to change you have to really want to. Then you have to gradually focus on those things which you can change, and chip away at them day by day. There is no instant magic answer.

Nevertheless, change is possible and is not necessarily difficult, but it requires a degree of commitment and patience. This course will lead you gently through the steps required, all you have to do is follow with an open mind.

That is where mindfulness comes in.

***

Test Yourself

(for those who want to check they understand so far)

1. *Which one thing is responsible for most of the negativity we all experience from time to time?*

2. *What is a 'head conversation'?*

3. *Before we can begin to change any bad habits what do we need to develop?*

4 – How to Develop Your Awareness

Mindfulness comes originally from Buddhism, but you don't have to be a Buddhist to practise it. These days the term 'mindfulness' is used in two different ways. In the first place it is often used to just refer to the meditation practices themselves. But the meditations are only half the story.

The second part of mindfulness is the philosophy. This entails a particular way of seeing the world which in most cases is far more helpful than our usual way. I am going to refer to each of these aspects of mindfulness in the course of this book and show how they can be helpful to you.

Mindfulness is made up of three major parts and we will be looking at each one and how it relates to the others and its relevance to everyday life. Sometimes the names given to these are slightly different but the meanings are the same. The first of these elements is Awareness.

There are also two slightly different concepts associated with awareness. The first of these is doing something "as if for the first time".

As If for the First Time

To understand this way of being aware think of somewhere you went for the very first time. For example, can you recall your first visit to a particular house, or arriving at a holiday destination that you'd never been to before?

On that first occasion you would have noticed lots of things, many details, smells, sounds, etc. Because it was all so new and different you noticed almost everything. Compare that to what you were noticing when you went to that same place, either at the end of the holiday or when you'd become accustomed to going there. By this time you would no longer be seeing all the details you saw on that first occasion.

I recall that on my first day at grammar school I was feeling very unsure as, wearing my brand new uniform, I made my way up the long, imposing driveway towards a long red brick building. I wasn't anxious, simply uncertain as I didn't know what to expect. Everything looked imposing.

Not ever having been there before my brain was wary because it hadn't proved the place to be safe.

On the day I left for the last time, seven years later, I remembered that first day. I turned and looked back.

Although the buildings were exactly the same, they now looked different to me. There were certain thoughts and feelings associated with various parts of the building. It no longer looked imposing and scary. I no longer 'saw' it in the same way as I had that first time.

The more familiar we are with something, the more we come to focus on just those aspects which are usually relevant to us and cease to 'see' the rest.

If you were to visit a town as a tourist, you'd probably notice as many details as you could. For instance, you'd look up at the parts of buildings above your eye-line, as well as in the shop windows. Compare that to being in the high street where you usually shop. It's quite likely that if I showed you a picture of that very high street but only depicting the upper storeys of the buildings, you wouldn't recognise it.

That's because when you go to the high street you go for a purpose—to shop. Therefore, only the shop windows are relevant. You have 'taught' your brain that the rest is surplus to the task in hand—to doing the shopping—so your attention is not unnecessarily drawn to it.

This is what happens as familiarity develops in any situation. We move away from seeing everything, towards only noticing what we have come to regard as relevant.

Brains work by linking things. They are also obsessed with keeping danger at bay because they have a survival instinct buried within. There are two sets of circumstances which alert the survival instinct.

First, any situation which has at any time in the past caused you to feel negative (pain, fear, sadness, etc.) This would seem quite logical and most people recognize when this is happening. For example, if you have recently been involved in a road traffic accident you would not be surprised to find that you felt somewhat anxious getting into a car again.

The second set of circumstances for which the survival instinct tends to become wary and raise your arousal somewhat, is those situations which it hasn't experienced previously. If it has never experienced them it doesn't know the outcome or, more importantly, whether they are safe. Therefore, to hedge its bets, it will put you slightly on your guard just in case . . .

Common examples of this are found when you maybe go for an interview. Because you don't know what to expect, up goes your arousal a bit. Many people then add to this by imagining worst case scenarios!

Once you have been there before, or done that, the survival instinct has past experience to go on. Therefore if the situation didn't prove dangerous the first time round it will not raise your arousal level quite so much the next time. This continues each time you have that same experience until eventually you can do it quite calmly.

Your brain also tries to be helpful. It takes note of what you pay attention to each time you experience a situation and directs your focus there the next time. This causes us to narrow down our awareness of what we consciously notice that isn't directly relevant in everyday situations.

For example, I would guess that almost every time you return home, as you enter you do the same things. That is what your brain has come to expect and what it will direct you towards. If the first thing you do is take off your shoes and put on your slippers that is what you may have come to find yourself doing almost on auto-pilot. If you always put your keys down somewhere, that is where you will put them without even realizing you're doing it.

You will also tend to notice what you always notice and disregard the rest. That is why when people are trying to sell their homes it is advisable to get someone unfamiliar with it to cast an eye over it and see it as a stranger would see it.

Possibly whenever you arrive home you are hungry so your mind locks onto the kitchen and what you might have to eat the moment you go through the front door. Your brain sees no point in noticing the scuff marks on the wall or the pile of newspapers on and under the table. It has learnt that this information is not relevant at that moment.

So another way of becoming more mindfully aware is to behave as if you are doing something for the first time and take none of the details for granted

In the Moment

That toddler in the previous chapter whom we imagined watching whilst it built a tower of bricks was 'in the moment'. The child was focusing all its awareness on that task. It wasn't wondering what it would have for tea, or why it couldn't have bigger or more colourful bricks. It was concentrating totally on the task in hand.

Furthermore, if the pile of bricks fell down, the child might cry in frustration. If it did it was not because it considered itself a failure or that it hadn't done it right. The child would cry because the lovely pile had suddenly gone and it was no longer gaining pleasure from seeing it there. In other words, everything that the child was experiencing was directly related to those bricks.

How often do grown-ups lose themselves in activities in this way? Sometimes, but more often, whatever we do, we either have our thoughts elsewhere, or we're commenting on what we're doing in our heads. In that case we are also often judging whether or not our performance is good enough in some way or other. This is not mindful.

I'm not saying here that we need to go through each and every day being totally mindfully aware. There are occasions when this would be inappropriate. For now I am simply encouraging you to develop your skill at doing it so that later you can do it when it's useful or helpful to do so.

This is where learning to meditate in a very short and simple way is helpful. Unlike toddlers and animals, the rest of we humans, by the time we reach adulthood, have become far too proficient at thinking. We do it constantly whether it's necessary or not.

Naturally, being creatures of habit, our brains have learnt that because we have tended to think about certain sorts of things in certain situations, they will now prompt us to keep doing just that in an effort to be helpful. And so we all struggle when we try not to think.

I will return to the concept of struggle in a later chapter. For now, the next most useful step is to start to learn ways of putting your mind where you want it to be as opposed to where it thinks or has learnt you want it to be. This is a skill so, like any skill, it will take time and practice to become good at it.

***

Test Yourself

1. There are three parts to mindfulness. Which is the first?

2. What does it mean to be 'in the moment'?

3. Who or what are naturally good at being 'in the moment'?

5 – Learn To Meditate on Touch

Many books and CDs on meditation will advise that you maybe sit on the floor, or use a meditation stool when meditating. Either of these is fine but not necessary for our purposes here. I am attempting to show you how you can use ways to meditate during normal everyday life.

For this reason I have devised meditations during which you can remain as inconspicuous as possible. Waiting rooms are often useful places to practise your meditation skills as you generally have little else to do but wait. You can also do them on public transport, sitting at your desk at work, whilst having a shower . . . The possibilities are simple and endless.

My suggestions for practising would not go down too well if I demanded that you get down on the floor and sit cross-legged.

The aim of meditation is not to relax your body as you may have learnt to do if you have attended specific relaxation classes or used recordings to this end. Mindful meditation is not about trying to do anything. It is simply about just being.

In our groups we ask that participants sit as upright as they can without causing themselves undue discomfort. We also allow people to keep their eyes open if they wish.

I would advise you to practise the meditation techniques both with your eyes open and with them closed. That way you will learn to apply the technique without having to close your eyes when you are in a public place, such as your GP's waiting room, should you choose to.

I personally find that when I choose to keep my eyes open I just stare at the floor rather than looking at anything in particular.

The best way to learn meditation is by doing it. The best way to do it at first is to simply follow instructions given by someone else. Once you know what is involved you can just do it without any instructions at all—you will understand better what I mean by that once you have got the hang of it.

There is a 2 minute 8 second recording of the first meditation—Brief Touch—which can be downloaded from the link found at the back of this book.

The instructions are included as part of the meditation. At the end of each meditation track you will hear a chime which tells you that the meditation is over.

I suggest you do this before reading further.

***

After Brief Touch

An important point to realise about all the meditations is that you are not expected to get through them without catching yourself thinking at some point(s). Beginners often get annoyed with themselves because their minds keep wandering off.

Your mind will most definitely have wandered off but did you get annoyed by this when it happened? Or were you able to just do as I said and lead your attention back to whatever I was talking about at the time?

The aim of mindful meditation is just to become aware when your mind wanders off, and then, without getting annoyed with yourself, placing it back where it's meant to be.

The relevance of being able to do this for everyday life is simple. As we have seen, almost all negative feelings we have now are caused by our thoughts. By means of our thoughts we introduce negative reminders of things past or anxious warnings about things which might come in the future, rather than keeping our minds full of what is actually happening at the time.

We have the power to change the way we feel now, if we can first become consciously aware that we are thinking unhelpful thoughts, and learn to let them go. Letting them go is where the meditation practices come in.

Mindfulness is a skill. The more you practise the easier it becomes as your brain starts expecting you to do it at certain times and in certain places so will start to suggest you do it. The more it slips naturally into your normal way of being, the greater the benefit you will derive from it.

You can't get away with only reading this book and understanding what it's about. You have to put it in action, you have to do it. You have to make it part of your regular daily life. If you do that, it will reward you. And for those of you who still say they don't have time, I say to you, 'Don't you ever use the toilet?'.

There is always an opportunity to meditate for half a minute, if you really have a mind to do it. If you can't find the time then you don't want it enough so you may as well give up now and stop kidding yourself.

Mindfulness, however, is more than the total focus which is used by small children and animals, as the following story shows.

***

The Monkey and Banana

A man wanted to catch a monkey. He found a coconut, cut it in half and removed the milk and flesh. Then he cut a small hole in one half of the shell. He attached the other half of the shell to a tree trunk using a piece of wire. Next he placed a small banana inside the other piece of shell and glued the shell back together. Leaving the shell attached to the tree trunk he hid and waited.

After a while along came a monkey. It saw the fruit inside the coconut and reached its hand in to get it, only to find that the hole was not big enough for its hand to come out again whilst grasping the fruit. The monkey didn't accept that its hand would not come back through the hole whilst grasping the banana and remained there struggling with it. Whilst the monkey was thus engrossed, the man came out of his hiding place and grabbed it.

All the monkey had to do to be free was let go!

***

Which would have been the case had it been fully mindful and aware of what it was doing. But its brain took over and told it that when it found a banana it must eat it. So the monkey just lapsed into its usual habit, not looking beyond it.

Awareness is only the first element to learn on the road to becoming truly mindful.

***

Action Points

1. *Practise the technique taught so far for a day or two before reading on. Practise keeping your mind in the moment, just as we did during 'Brief Touch'. You can either continue to practise using the download or you can just do it without.*

2. *As you go about your daily life, as well as practising thirty second meditations, keep noticing those times when you indulge in 'head conversations'. At this stage you don't have to do anything about them, this is only the awareness stage.*

When you do the washing up is your mind elsewhere?

When you are washing in the shower are your thoughts on what's next or are you worrying about something that happened earlier?

When you eat your food, are you aware of the taste or is your head full of other matters?

6 – Does Your Alarm System Need a

Service?

Why do we always find it so hard to change our habits even when it would be to our advantage?

Picture yourself sitting at home watching TV. There's a bowl of fruit close by and, while engrossed in your programme, you reach out and pick up an apple. You then proceed to eat the apple while watching the programme. I'll bet that for the most part you aren't consciously aware of how that particular apple tastes or feels in your mouth. Your attention is on the TV. You may even eat the entire apple without really being aware you've eaten it, just as smokers often smoke their cigarettes without noticing what they're doing.

However, if, by some misfortune, that apple has a large bruise which you hadn't noticed to begin with, as you get a bruised mouthful you suddenly become aware of the taste and your attention switches from the TV to the apple. You may even spit it out and study it to see why the taste was suddenly so unexpected. On the other hand, if the apple is flawless, its perfection will pass unnoticed. So why is this?

From the moment of birth our senses—sight, hearing, touch, smell and taste—are picking up information from our environment. If we were constantly fully consciously aware of all this information, we'd have brain overload!

Think for a moment how often we deliberately cut off some of this information so as to focus on one sort of input specifically. For instance, we may close our eyes in order to concentrate on sound while listening to music. When eating something special we may close our eyes in order to focus on the taste.

If we were constantly fully aware of all the input, we wouldn't be able to do anything else at all. There would be no brain space left to think about work or anything.

Nature must have realised this and so it built into each of us an alarm system. To this part of us the world is a big, potentially dangerous, place. It works a bit like the burglar alarm monitor you may have in your home or have seen in others. It has to spot danger even before we become consciously aware of it and alert us to it before the danger gets us. That's its job. And it works really well, albeit too well in many cases.

But how does it know what's dangerous?

To the alarm system everything is guilty until proved innocent. Therefore anything which has caused us to feel a negative emotion in the past, anything that previously made us feel, for example, pain, fear, embarrassment, or anxiety, sets the alarm ringing.

Not only that, but the alarm is also triggered by anything we've never come across before, anything new or different. If it has never come across it before it doesn't know it will prove to be safe, so warns us anyway by raising our awareness generally.

Sometimes when our awareness is raised in this way we enjoy it and interpret the feeling as curiosity or interest. That is what is happening when we visit a place as a tourist as described on page 56.

This automatically-raised awareness is felt in varying degrees when we encounter anything different from what we're used to, even if it's potentially pleasant. Sometimes we interpret the feeling as anxiety or apprehension.

Perhaps you have noticed that you felt a little bit uneasy on reaching a new foreign holiday destination. You may even have become aware of this and wondered why, when you were supposed to be on holiday, relaxing. But given what we've just discussed regarding the alarm system, this is quite normal. At your new destination the air, the smells, the sounds are totally new to the alarm system, so it raises your awareness just in case . . .

So for everything that comes up, the brain first of all tries to match it to something it already knows. If it can identify it in this way and the match isn't something that proved dangerous in the past, it lets it by.

That is why you stop seeing all the features of your high street when you're shopping and just notice the relevant bits, as described in 'as if for the first time' (page 54). To see that in action let's now go back to the apple you were eating while watching TV.

When you first took that apple from the fruit bowl, your alarm system immediately trawled its memory and came up with a 'script' for that apple. It found a match because you'd eaten an apple very much like that many times before and presumably liked it otherwise you wouldn't be choosing to eat another now.

So your brain now assumed how it would taste, how it would smell, how it would feel in your mouth, etc. And provided that your actual experience matched what it expected, your attention wouldn't be drawn to what you were eating. This would leave you free to continue to focus on your TV programme at the same time.

On the other hand, when you bit into the large bruise your brain immediately realised that it was no longer experiencing what it expected and would instantly take your attention away from the TV to the apple, causing you to spit it out.

It is now very likely that the next time you go to eat an apple you will check that it doesn't have any nasty bits first. If the experience was particularly unpleasant you may even be reluctant to eat more apples. If this happens it is because the alarm is seeing the apple and giving you a strong warning. How you respond to this will determine whether the warning gets dismissed, or gets even stronger the next time.

Whenever we do what our brains tell us to do we are creating habits. The more often we do these, the more entrenched they become. Sometimes we want to unlearn these. We often try to do this by trying to block out what our brains are trying to tell us to do. This doesn't work.

When you try to block something or distract yourself from it, you are actually focusing on it even more! The trick to getting rid of thoughts you don't want is by leaving them where they are and simply moving your awareness elsewhere.

That is the basis of meditation.

You probably won't be able to do that just yet, but the skill will come if you just keep practising a little each day.

If you keep practising you will find that it becomes enjoyable.

The 'Brief Touch' meditation focused on showing you how to become mindful of touch. When doing a meditation, touch is only one of the many possible things you could choose to focus on. I introduce it first because most people find it easiest

In the course of this book I will attempt to show you various other possibilities. There is no single right thing that you must focus on when meditating as you will realise. It's for you to use whichever is best for you at the time. It may be that you tend always to choose the same one, it may be that you always do it differently. That doesn't matter. For now I invite you to do another exercise.

ACTION POINT:

As you're reading this I very much doubt whether you're consciously aware of the feel of your clothes against your skin—unless you're wearing something very different or uncomfortable.

You will possibly have now become aware, simply because I've drawn your attention to it by mentioning it, but only because of that.

Pause for a moment and consciously check out the input of your five senses (sight, hearing, touch, taste, smell) one by one.

If you wish make a note of your observations. See if you can describe the sensations rather than just labelling them.

For example if I asked, "What can you hear?" Most of us would tend to just label what we hear and would write something like this:

"I can hear lorries and cars passing on the motorway. Every now and then there's a break in the traffic and then another lorry goes by . . ."

Or maybe:

"I hear birds singing in the garden. Every now and then the dog changes its position. In the background the clock on the mantelpiece is ticking . . ."

But neither of these descriptions actually describes the sounds you're hearing. What you are doing is labelling those sounds according to what your brain is telling you is making them.

How does it know what is making them? It has matched the sounds you are hearing with other records in its memory banks and found what it thinks is a match. I want you to describe the sensations themselves rather than what your brain tries to tell you is causing them.

In order to do that you might write something like the following:

"I hear deep rumbling sounds and now and then there are higher-pitched ones. From time to time there's silence and a shooshing before another rumbling . . ."

Or maybe:

"There's a high-pitched musical sound further away. The sound goes up and down the octave for a bit then pauses. Nearer is an occasional rustling sound. Closest to me I hear a rhythmic and constant clicking . . ."

This is what I mean by describing the sensation itself.

Now you try it . . . You may want to get a piece of paper to write own your descriptions . . .

What do you hear?

. . . .

What do you taste?

. . . .

*What do you feel (in terms of touch sensations **not** emotions)?*

. . . .

What can you smell?

....

***

Notice that I haven't invited you to deliberately observe what you see. This is because those of us who are not visually impaired tend to allow sight to dominate our other four senses. We judge our world firstly by how it looks and may often come to false conclusions as a result.

To demonstrate this, imagine that someone has just placed a plate of food in front of you. It smells of curry, which is your favourite food. If you were blindfolded, your mouth would water at the smell and you would in all probability be prepared to taste it. Suppose, however, that this particular plate of food, although it smells like curry, is coloured bright blue. Would you still be longing to taste it?

If you were still wearing the blindfold you probably would. If you took the blindfold off and saw the blue curry then you might not.

Once we have experienced a particular situation, our alarm system has recorded the script. Each time we then encounter that same situation, or a similar one, the same script replays automatically and so we experience the same emotion again. In the case of a pleasant memory this isn't usually a problem. In the case of some sort of negative experience, it can continue to give us bad emotion even when there is no logical reason for it.

This same old script will keep replaying. Every time it's replayed we once again experience some negative memory and emotion. This negative emotion tells the alarm system each time that this experience is still bad news, so the alarm system keeps it tagged as 'dangerous'.

And so we may continue to experience negative emotion about something which in reality is no more than a memory, but which, because it has a negative tag, keeps being re-experienced in the same way again and again. And it will continue to be experienced in this way until we make a conscious effort to change the script.

We will look further into how this affects us in the next lesson. But there's enough new information to practise for today.

1. Woman looks at calendar
2. Brain links date with something bad that happened once
3. Brain makes link between what happened and emotion
4. Woman feels sad

***

Action Points

1. Keep practising being mindful of touch for 20 or 30 seconds at odd moments throughout the day. You can listen again to the 'brief touch' download if you wish.

2. Eat or drink at least one thing mindfully. This can be something small—a chip, a biscuit, a swig of tea— something you were going to have anyway. When you eat or drink mindfully you focus all your attention on what it is and notice the sensations it makes as it's in your mouth, how it feels on your tongue, against your teeth, and as you swallow it.

It is very important that you remember to carry out these small exercises a few times in the course of your normal day. This is how you learn to make mindfulness a part of your life. If you practise in this small way, it will be effortless, but you have to bother to do it. I suggest that you spend a day or two re-reading to here and familiarising yourself with the lessons learnt so far before continuing with the next lesson.

***

Test Yourself

1. What does the alarm system regard as dangerous?

2. What happens if you don't respond with a negative feeling (fear, anxiety, sadness) when the alarm system warns you about something?

7 – How To Meditate on Sound

This meditation is about sound. Have you ever noticed that we tend to label sound which we find pleasant as 'music' whereas that which we dislike is often termed 'noise'. Both music and noise are sound.

Consider for a moment that classic scenario when you go to bed at night only to realise that the neighbours are having a party. You lie in bed telling yourself that you're trying to sleep, but in fact you're listening for the noise from next door to stop. Each time there's a pause in the music you possibly prick up your ears in the hope that it has stopped, only to be downcast a moment later when the next track starts.

Assuming that you have decided, for whatever reason, that getting out of bed, going next door and asking them to turn the noise down isn't advisable, you lie tossing and turning, monitoring every break in the noise in the hope that it's stopping. The next day you will no doubt complain of being tired because you were kept awake by the party next door. That is not the case.

In actual fact it wasn't the noise next door which prevented you from falling asleep. What stopped you sleeping was the fact that you were focusing your attention on the constant stopping and starting of the sounds from next door. You were constantly thinking about them, focusing on them.

Because you were also experiencing a degree of agitation, irritation, or other negative emotion, your alarm system was ensuring you kept paying attention. Let us look at the way mindfulness deals with situations such as this.

It is possible for a human being to sleep through any amount of ongoing noise but, because most of us have trained ourselves not to, we find it impossible. Babies sleep through noise. When my own children were babies I would occasionally deliberately start vacuuming, or would put the crib near to the washing machine if they were fractious and needing to sleep. The repetitive machine sounds would lull them to sleep.

Why was this? Simply because, unable to think in words about how annoying the noise is etc. the baby gives up resisting the sound and so falls asleep. It accepts what it doesn't have the power to change.

The reason we, as adults, find it difficult to sleep when there's a party next door is merely because we start to focus on the source of irritation and resist it by wishing it would stop. Were we able to just notice what was happening, shrug and focus on our own thoughts of something pleasant instead, the sound wouldn't prevent us sleeping.

Practising meditation using any focus helps us to learn how to better control our own minds and so enables us to place them where we want them rather than where circumstances dictate they will go. The meditation on sound is just a further example which can be used as practice.

In everyday life this is a good focus for meditation when you are somewhere in nature which is reasonably peaceful, such as on a secluded beach, in your own garden in the summer, whilst walking in the country etc.

When you meditate on sound you are not aiming to identify what's making the sound you hear. Nevertheless, most of the time, at least to begin with, your ever-helpful brain will provide you with pictures of what it thinks is making the noise, provided it has actually come across a similar noise previously. If, however, it has never encountered such a noise before and has nothing about it in its memory store it will either come up with the nearest thing, or, regard it as potentially dangerous and try to warn you about it.

A tip I have found useful when learning to meditate on sound is to keep my eyes closed and picture one of those digital sound level monitors. These jump up and down according to the frequency and volume of sound as it's being recorded. To imagine this helps me to focus on the quality of the sound itself as opposed to what might be making it.

So sit and play the brief sound meditation (2 minutes 48 seconds) download from the link at the back of the book.

8 – Stop the Negative Past Colouring

Now

Previously we considered how our brains, and in particular the alarm system's automatic programming, actually affect how we see the world moment by moment. This is possibly the most important lesson to understand in the whole of this book as it explains why bad memories and habits are not so easy to get rid of.

Imagine that part of your brain is made up of a huge hall containing hundreds of filing cabinets. Picture too dozens of little people (imaginary) who work in this hall as filing clerks. From the moment of birth these filing clerks go into action. Anything and everything you experience is sent to be filed somewhere in these filing cabinets.

Each time you experience anything at all, from waking up in the morning to finding a cow eating your back lawn (this has happened to me but it was many cows not just one), a message is sent from the alarm system to the filing clerks saying, "What's this?" The filing clerks then run around at very high speed to retrieve from the files any information about that experience that is already stored and send it back to the alarm system in head office to process.

If the information that comes back is not negative in any way, the alarm system will tell the brain it's ok and not to panic. It will also tell it what to expect. Let us consider an example.

You wake up in the morning in your own bed as usual. This input is received by the filing clerks who easily match it because it is ready to hand for them in the "normal everyday happenings" file. This all happens so fast that you'd not be aware of it. Because the information is exactly what is expected you don't get any alarm warnings so don't feel the slightest degree of anxiety. However, when you stagger downstairs and notice the cow on the lawn, the response may be different.

If this hasn't happened before the filing clerks won't be able to provide the alarm system with any information as to what to expect. The alarm system will therefore be forced to issue a danger warning and you may then feel a degree of anxiety or discomfort as a result. How you then respond will determine how the incident gets filed for the future.

Therefore if you just shrug and go and phone the farmer, the incident will be filed as "not a problem" and the next time it happens you will be unlikely to get a danger warning from the alarm system. If, however, you are terrified of cows and panic, the incident will be filed as "dangerous" and you will be given a very real warning and will become panicky much quicker as a result should it happen again.

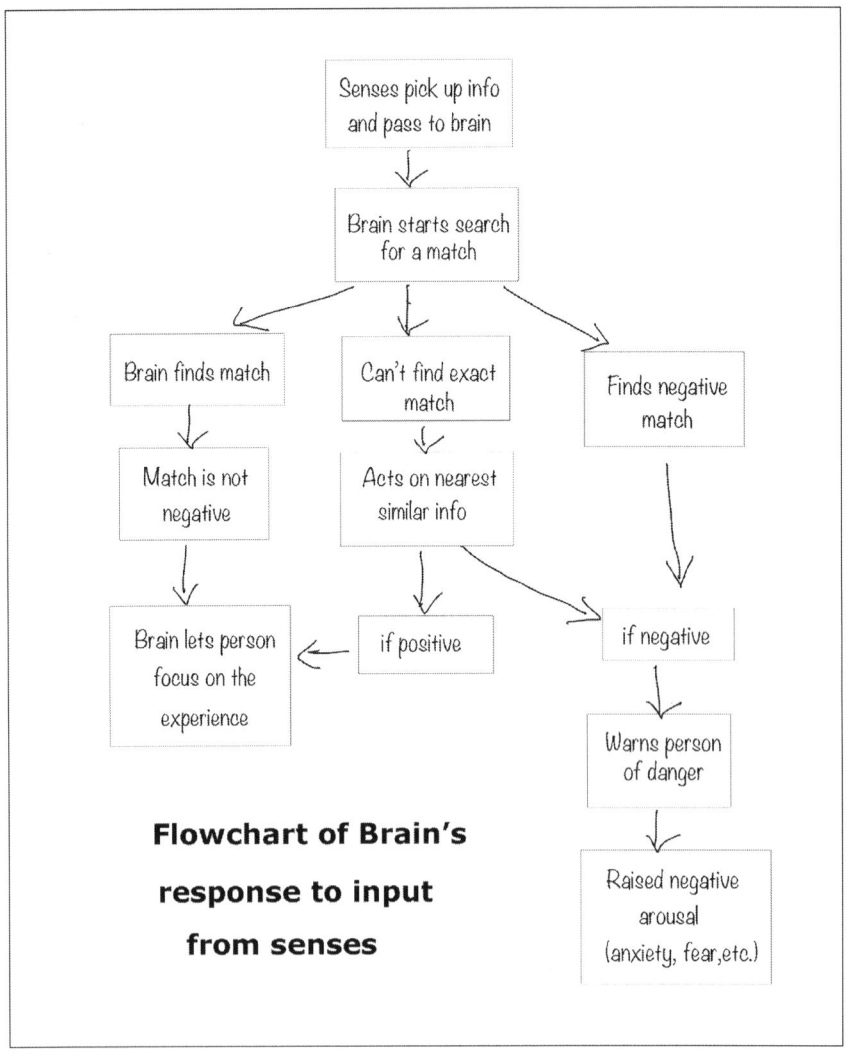

Flowchart of Brain's response to input from senses

Consider now that scenario when you were eating the apple and bit into a bruised bit. Most probably the act of eating an apple will now have been tagged as "potentially dangerous" by the filing clerks. As a result, the next time you pick one up to eat, something will probably prompt you to look carefully at it first. It may be that you will then have to eat several apples that are ok before you stop getting that warning each time you go to eat one.

What I have tried to do with this lengthy explanation is make you realise that we all normally experience our present life through a filter made up of what has happened in the past. When what has happened in the past has been pleasant or neutral, this isn't a problem. Where it becomes more relevant, however, is if the past was negative in any way.

What if, as a small child, you fell into a pond and became very frightened for a short time before you were rescued. That incident was filed away until the next time you came near to a similar expanse of water, whereupon the alarm system would jump in and warn you.

As it issues its warnings it reminds you of the past images and feelings. This is similar to actually having that original experience all over again. You feel that same anxiety which now attaches itself to this present situation as well. Thus your fear of being near water gains strength each time you are near any, even when there is no real danger at all.

When I was a young child I had two minor accidents at home—one when I was two and the other when I was five. Both involved quite a lot of blood. What made it worse was the fact that my mother was squeamish and didn't react well. As a small child I must've picked up on some of my mother's anxiety and this only added to the amount of negative emotion (fear) that I experienced. There was also a painful follow-on to the second accident which added to what my alarm system was recording.

As a result of these experiences I grew up with a very negative association to accidents involving blood. I would quickly feel faint if I saw anything more than the mildest scratch. What was even worse was that I could even imagine gory scenes and start to feel faint as a result.

This over-active imagination was at the root of the panic attacks which I experienced for almost thirty years, until I retrained my mind to react differently to the triggers.

We don't experience 'now' for what it is. We experience it through the filter of our past until we learn to do differently. We leave our brains on automatic to process nearly all of our everyday information as shown in the flowchart diagram (page98).

As a result of this we usually get automated responses based on whatever has happened to us in the past. These very often bear absolutely no relationship to what is actually going on here and now. Most of us will benefit hugely if we learn to turn off the auto-pilot sometimes and make the decisions for ourselves.

That is where mindfulness training comes in useful. When we feel negative about 'now' it's nearly always because those old filed reports from the past are being referred to, rather than being due to any real threat in the present moment. As I said at the start, if there was a real threat you'd be actively dealing with it and not spending time wondering about how you were feeling.

The purpose of the Action Point described on page 80, which invited you to describe what your senses were picking up in a particular way, was to teach you to see things for what they actually are now. It asked you to avoid describing the sensations in the way you would normally (in terms of what was making them), and to focus on other attributes of those same sensations.

I will give some examples from my own experiences.

When I was a young child my parents had few visitors to the house. Therefore, when my uncles or aunts did visit, my sister and I would be excited. I recall that we always tried to be on our best behaviour initially, but as the visit wore on, the excitement increased and we became more and more boisterous. After the visitors had gone home my sister and I nearly always got a good talking-to from my father for being silly.

In adult life I used to be very quiet when visitors came to my home, almost to the point of being unsociable. Then one day I realised that the emotion I was feeling just before visitors arrived was the same as that I had as a child, when I was afraid of incurring the disapproval of my father. Even though my father was no longer alive, I was still feeling anxious at the prospect of visitors and afraid of being extroverted in their presence.

Once I became aware of this, I was able to challenge it and make a conscious effort to change the way I felt and behaved. By doing this each time, I eventually lost the tendency to feel anxious about visitors. I had rewritten the script stored in my brain's filing hall.

Not all our automatic scripts come from childhood. The brain adapts very readily and you may find that you have scripts which were far more recently written. I am currently in the process of rewriting a script of my own which has been preventing me from achieving things which I really wanted to do. I will attempt to describe how it came about.

I had often found myself wanting desperately to become engrossed in doing a painting or even writing this book, but was unable to 'get down to it'. I caught myself doing all manner of minor chores first to such a degree that days would pass without any progress. I questioned my own hidden motives. Was I afraid of failing etc.?

None of the explanations I came up with seemed to ring true. In the end I realised that the problem was an old script from the time when I had five children to bring up.

In those days, although I often had an hour here or there in which to indulge my hobbies, I rarely had longer before I had to cook a meal, take someone somewhere, and so on. One of my strong personality traits has always been that I'm an all-or-nothing sort of person. If I get into something I lose myself in it completely and hate to be interrupted. If I can't do that then I usually don't bother at all.

Before I had any children I would become engrossed in a creative pursuit and would continue for hours on end. I recalled that in the early days of child-rearing I used to attempt this, but would keep having to drag myself away prematurely in order to do some domestic task. This resulted in my feeling frustrated. To avoid this negative emotion I chose to just focus on the children and household tasks for the time being. I filled my time instead with little projects, such as baking cakes, which I had time to complete.

The children all grew up and left many years ago but recently I realised that it was that same script which had been holding me back of late. I was still getting that feeling of impending frustration when I considered starting something that I wanted to focus on. My brain would think, "I know this situation," and would throw up all the feelings which it had come to associate with my becoming deeply engrossed in anything .

These underlying feelings, usually of frustration, would then be enough to distract me and cause me to feel reluctant to start, but without my being aware of what was happening or questioning it. All I did was react to the feeling by avoiding doing what I really wanted to do.

Now that I have realised that script was there, I have been able to consciously overcome it, and am beginning once again to lose myself in projects—such as writing this.

This is a typical example of the way in which old scripts get replayed by the brain and cause us to feel emotion which belongs to that old script but which is not necessarily helpful or relevant to the situation in hand. Once we start to become aware of these old scripts and when they get played, we can start to change the way we feel about things.

In the case of scripts which evoke pleasant memories, such as a happy feeling you always get when you visit a particular seaside town because it reminds you of childhood holidays, you may not want to change them. That's fine. The scripts most of us want to change are those which evoke negative emotions of one kind or another. What mindfulness offers is the ability to change those things you want to change.

Changes can be stressful

At this point I must warn you about how changes may make you feel, even when they are positive changes.

Remember that the alarm system bases what's safe on things it's familiar with and which have been proved not to be dangerous in the past. By the same token, anything which is different and which you haven't come across before is regarded to begin with as possibly dangerous. The alarm system will raise your awareness just in case.

Therefore, when you make changes to your normal way of doing things, don't be surprised if you feel a little uneasy at first. As long as you don't become anxious about feeling that way, it will soon fade. I experienced a perfect example of this happening when I was in my teens.

Some of the girls in my class at school came from very musical backgrounds and knew a lot about classical music. I knew next to nothing and felt I wanted to know more. I persuaded my mother to buy some classical LPs. I was particularly drawn to Beethoven because I'd been taught to play a few short pieces of his in my piano lessons.

In those days if there was a record player in the home it would be in the main lounge. Therefore I had to wait my chance to indulge in this new learning. One evening when my parents had gone out I settled down on the settee and played the Beethoven LP.

The record sleeve told me what each movement was conveying. I followed this as I listened. Although I enjoyed the music, by the end of it I became aware that I was feeling somewhat uneasy. In order to get rid of the feeling I felt I had to play a pile of my usual/familiar pop records and sing along to them. This helped me feel at ease again.

The discomfort I had felt was caused by doing  something which I did not usually do when home alone. I was attempting to change what was normal for me. Once I reverted to my usual behaviour everything felt fine once more. I gradually got used to listening to the classical music by only playing it for very short periods of time to begin with, rather than an entire evening.

The point of that little story is that change to everyday routine may feel uncomfortable at first. This is why the more familiar you are with what you are trying to change, the more gradually you must put it into practice and the more reassurance you will need to give yourself as you do it.

That is why people who are trying to stop smoking may find it particularly hard. Smokers usually associate having a cigarette with feeling good. They also often link smoking with certain times of the day, at the end of a meal for instance. When they attempt not to smoke, not only are they having to combat the addictive cravings, they are also having to contend with changes to familiar routine and especially routines which generally serve to calm them or make them feel good in some way.

Therefore if you were going to give up smoking it might be an idea to break the familiarity habit first by deliberately changing where and when you smoke. Once you have eliminated that part of the habit, you only have the cravings to contend with as you stop smoking altogether. (Those few lines are not intended as a comprehensive guide to giving up smoking. I have only included them to demonstrate the point.)

Some of you may be disagreeing with me now because you don't generally feel unease at doing some of the things I've just mentioned. That may well be the case. We are not all born equal in the speed at which we react to warnings of our alarm systems.

Why laid-back people don't often get anxious

Some people inherit a very slow-moving arousal system. Such people get a warning and only feel mildly concerned. They look around to see what the problem is, notice that there's no real danger, switch off the warning with a mental shrug, and go back to what they were doing. You can probably name someone you know who is just like that—so laid-back that they're almost horizontal all the time.

If you are one of these, it's very unlikely you'll be reading this book because you just don't see what the problem is, because for you there isn't one!

When the alarm system gives a warning which is disregarded, it learns that the warning is unnecessary and so stops bothering to give it. Once the laid-back person has switched off in this way, they won't be bothered by that again.

At the other extreme there are those who inherit a very quick-acting arousal system. These people get a warning and then start to worry about what the problem might be, start focusing on how bad, how anxious or down, they feel. The alarm system interprets this as being proved right and makes sure that the warnings keep coming.

Because laid-back people rarely react with anxiety when they receive warnings from the alarm system, they have far fewer "dangerous" incidents recorded in their filing halls in the course of their lives. It follows then that they also have fewer potential warning triggers too.

People who react to the alarm system warnings with anxiety or fear are ensuring that the incident will be filed as "dangerous" in their filing halls. It follows then that if you can become aware of such warnings and learn to dismiss them sooner as not posing a problem, you will not be filing as many potential warnings for the future. Mindfulness can help you to do this.

It's not what happens to us that causes us problems but how we think about what happens.

And now another story to reflect on . . .

***

The Tiger and the Stawberry

A man went out for a walk one afternoon. He walked along smelling the air, feeling the breeze on his skin, aware of the ground beneath his feet. After a while he paused to glance back and noticed, far in the distance, a tiger, who was also out for a stroll.

The man quickened his pace a little and went a little

further. He looked back again and saw that the tiger too had quickened its pace.

The man began to jog. After a few more paces a glance

over his shoulder revealed that the tiger too had begun to jog.

The man broke into a run. He looked back and saw that the tiger was now bounding forwards, gaining on him. The man was now running flat out . . . so was the tiger.

Suddenly, to his horror, the man found he was at the edge of a cliff with a sheer drop before him. He looked back and the tiger was still coming. For a moment the man was panic-stricken, then he noticed that there was a vine growing down the cliff-face. The tiger was getting closer.

The man grabbed the vine and began climbing down the cliff. After a while, he glanced up and there was the tiger peering down at him. The man looked down to see how much further he had to go . . . and there at the bottom stood a second tiger gazing up at him.

The man looked back at the top and was shocked to see that the first tiger was now chewing through the vine. Then the man noticed that growing in a crevice just to his right was a wild strawberry plant. On this plant was one *luscious ripe red strawberry. The man reached out a hand, picked the strawberry and enjoyed it.*

***

What did you experience as you read the last sentence?

Whenever I have told this story during a course I am met with a stunned silence. Everyone appears to be waiting for a different punchline. Everyone seems to expect the man to be rescued at the last moment.

It is possible that suddenly the cavalry arrived and shot the tiger. That would be the man's good fortune . . . but he was powerless to make that happen.

To all intents and purposes the man was powerless to change what was to be his fate. Therefore he chose instead to focus on something which he did have power to control . . . He chose to experience the pleasure of eating a strawberry.

This brings us to the next element of Mindfulness which we will explore in the next chapter.

***

Action Points

1. *Keep practising the brief meditations focusing on touch. For example:*

(i) You could now try doing this maybe while doing the washing up. Here you focus on the feel of the water, on watching the surfaces of the dishes become clean, on the smell of the soap suds . . . etc.

(ii) Another possibility is to focus on the sensations you experience whilst cleaning your teeth. How does the brush feel in different areas? Be aware of the sensations in your gums, on the surfaces of your teeth, on your tongue or lips . . .

(iii) Then there's the shower or bath. Allow yourself to focus on the sensations in your skin as you wash it. Be aware of the feel of the water against different parts of your body.

Whichever exercises you do, focus just on the sensations. The idea is not to judge them in any way as good or bad but rather to simply notice them for what they are.

2. Start to become aware of those old filed reports colouring what you are experiencing in the here and now.

***

Test Yourself

1. Through what do we experience our present?

2. When you encounter something totally new, what determines whether it's filed as dangerous?

9 – What To Do When You Can't Do

Anything

As I said, whenever I've just told the tiger story in a Mindfulness group session I'm confronted by a roomful of puzzled and sometimes even horrified expressions. When I ask why this is I get responses such as:

"Couldn't he have thrown the strawberry at the tiger at the bottom and run away while it wasn't looking?" or, "Well, that's not a happy ending!"

Others just stare at me in disbelief that someone could eat at a time like that!

These reactions address issues which are very relevant to our everyday lives. I will return to the expectation of a happy ending in the next session. For now I want to talk about the inability of my audience to accept that someone could turn their attention to eating and enjoying a wild strawberry when about to die.

There are three basic components to Mindfulness as we teach it. The first is Awareness, which we have already considered in a previous chapter. The second component is Acceptance.

This usually starts a discussion because a lot of people seem to think that acceptance = giving in. That is not the case at all.

You have no doubt at some time come across the Prayer of Serenity which goes like this:

Lord, grant me the strength to change those things I can change.

The courage to accept those things I can't change.

And the wisdom to know the difference.

Mindfulness teaches us to choose to accept what we can't change, or have chosen not to change for one reason or another. Where most people come unstuck at first is that they seem not to be aware when they are trying to change something over which they have no power at all.

What causes most of us to experience negative feelings unnecessarily is our refusal to accept those things which we cannot change.

What Can We Control?

The main problem with control is not simply that we often attempt to control what isn't in our power. The main problem is that we appear not even to be aware that it's not in our power. This is what is behind the inability of the group participants mentioned at the start of the chapter, to accept the outcome of the tiger story. They are, without realising it, expecting the man to be able to save himself somehow. It is this expectation that is colouring their reaction to the ending.

There is only one thing in this life that you or I, or any one of us, no matter who we are, however wealthy, however poor, however powerful, however humble, truly has the potential to control. Furthermore, the control of that one thing rests with each one of us individually and nobody else. Nobody can take control of that one thing of yours unless you have given it to them, and they can only keep control of it for as long as you allow them to. What is it?

The answer is you and, more specifically, your thoughts.

You are ruled, as we have already seen in talking about past scripts, by your own thoughts, including patterns of behaviour which your brain has learnt as it went along and of which you may not be consciously aware. You are the only one who is able to control your thoughts. Other people may at times attempt to make you think in a certain way for various reasons . . . but they can only succeed at this if you allow it.

At this point I can almost hear various readers saying, "But I have to do such and such, even though I don't want to!" This is never true. You always have a choice. It's just that the available or possible choices aren't always the ones we'd like to have.

Let's consider the man who was holding onto the vine, halfway down the rock face. This man has choices. The one choice he doesn't have is for the tigers to just go away. He has no power to control what the tigers do. He is only able to control himself, his own thoughts and his own behaviour.

He realises he is going to die, unless matters out of his control change the circumstances. For instance, someone might appear out of nowhere and shoot one of the tigers. But that is not something he can influence. He can only work with what is in his power.

The one thing which he does have the power to control is his own thoughts and actions. He has choices, but not necessarily the choices he'd like to have!

He could, for example, just let go of the rope and fall. He could swing to and fro. He could toss the strawberry down for the tiger to eat as a sort of hors d'oeuvre. Or he could choose to focus his attention on something which is pleasant for him at this moment.

This is what he does when he enjoys the strawberry. His actions don't change the final outcome, but there was nothing in his power at that moment which would have done. So he uses his power to influence the way he feels, making it positive rather than negative.

He accepts what he has no power to change and focuses his attention in a positive direction instead.

It is the re-focusing on something positive, however small, which makes the difference between acceptance and 'giving up'. Mindfulness is about becoming aware of our own power and using it for our benefit.

Mindful acceptance is based on being aware of our options and actively choosing one of them. It is not a question of being forced into a position of feeling powerless and then giving up.

Resistance

Most of us spend a lot of time resisting. We fail to accept what we have no power to change. At the same time we are often wishing we had choices that simply don't exist. I call these the 'missing options'.

Once we learn awareness of the difference, we are able to focus our efforts on what is within our own power. The result of this is a greater feeling of wellbeing even when the odds may appear to an outsider to be stacked against us.

To use an everyday example, I have a friend who absolutely hates ironing, Because she dislikes it she tends to put it off again and again until she ends up doing it late on a Sunday night because her family need the clothes for work and school the following morning.

So she gets out the dreaded ironing board and plugs in the iron. She then stands, ironing, for the next two hours, all the time reminding herself how much she hates doing it and resenting the fact that she has to do it. This is resistance.

So what could she do? First she must consider her real choices.

Could she pay somebody else to do it? Let's assume she can't.

Could other members of the family do their own ironing? Perhaps they are capable, but they would refuse to do it.

Could she leave their things un-ironed? Probably not because then they would all go out in creased clothes and she feels that would reflect badly on her as a mother.

Could she do a little bit each day so there's not a pile on a Sunday evening? She never manages to do this although she has often made an attempt, but it has been short-lived as other things got in the way.

The missing option—the one which she'd like but which doesn't exist—is for the family to do their own ironing if she doesn't do it for them. But she knows that they don't really care as much as she does whether or not their clothes are ironed. So that isn't a real option.

A real option is one which is in her power to do.

So now that it seems the current option is the only one that is workable for her at the moment, there is nothing to be gained but stress by spending two hours a week at the ironing board feeling resentful.

Following the example of the man on the vine, she needs to focus on some pleasant aspect of what she is doing whilst ironing. She may choose to play some music and sing along, or iron to the music. I personally just enjoy watching the creases smoothed away.

For the most part our negative experience of life isn't the result of what happens to us, but is due to the way we think about what happens to us!

Since we are the only ones with the power to really control our thinking we have a potentially very powerful weapon here in the quest for our own wellbeing. When we cannot change what happens to us, we can change the way it affects us by changing the way we habitually think.

So acceptance is doing what's best for you under circumstances where you have to compromise or put up with something which would not be of your own choosing but which you're stuck with. Acceptance is not the same as being downtrodden. Acceptance is about not resisting what you have no power to control or change. This includes the thoughts and behaviours of others. It's about seeing the situation for what it really is, rather than wishing it were different. Let's consider an example.

I once knew a lady whom I'll call Beryl. For over twenty years she had lived with a husband who drank excessively. When drunk her would call her names and tell her how useless she was. He would also mess up the home.

In addition to this, Beryl had a mental illness on account of which she experienced bouts of depression from time to time. In her case, the bouts of depression were made worse by her domestic situation. For Beryl, the most damaging aspect of her husband's behaviour was the way in which he belittled her. As a result over the years she had lost all her self- confidence and self esteem.

Beryl did have choices, even though she wasn't aware she had. She had spent years in this situation wishing her husband would change and almost believing that it was her fault in some way that he treated her as he did. Her daily life was based around the fear that this was another day when he might come home drunk.

This constant anxiety made her feel less and less valued and her depression worse. She wouldn't leave him as she had nowhere else to go, was unable to get a job on account of her illness, and didn't want to leave her home.

When we did the session about acceptance and not resisting what you couldn't change or what was not in your power to change, it was as if someone turned on a light for Beryl. She stopped hoping that her husband would change and accepted him for the drunk he was.

She realised that only he could change his own behaviour and that, although it was unlikely that he would, if he ever did reform then that would just be a bonus. More importantly, she had to accept the reality for what it was now and act accordingly.

She also recognised that his belittling of her was just an expression of how he felt. She didn't have to behave as if it were true. She stopped allowing herself to feel guilty about her husband's behaviour as if she was to blame, and realised that if she had in some way contributed to it, then that was her husband's problem, not hers.

She learnt to stop spending her days worrying whether he might be drunk later and started focusing her thoughts instead on things which made her feel good. If he did come home drunk she'd just avoid him.

She learnt to stop listening to his taunts and thinking about them, and instead to merely hear them just as sound with no significance. She acknowledged to herself that she was choosing to stay with him because it suited her, rather than because she felt she had no other options.

None of Beryl's changes happened overnight but by the end of the course she was wearing a smile. She said she was now focusing her life around what made her feel good each day, rather than around her old beliefs about not deserving anything and her worries about how her husband might behave that night.

What had brought about this happiness? Her physical situation hadn't changed. She still lived in the same place. She still had her bouts of depressive illness. Her husband's behaviour hadn't changed. She had simply accepted what she couldn't change and changed what was in her power—her own thinking!

Nobody can be influenced by someone else's actions unless they allow themselves to be. Each of us is responsible for the way we allow ourselves to think about what happens to us, or what others do to us. This is why two people can experience an identical situation and one will get over it, whereas it may appear to affect the other for life.

At this point I can hear readers protesting that they can't help the way they feel. That may be true. The initial emotion evoked by something is fairly automatic. What makes the difference, however, is whether we become aware of how that emotion is affecting us or not.

A prime example of this is the habit which some people have (and especially characters in TV soaps) of becoming depressed and despondent on the anniversary of someone's death. It works like this. The date itself is often the trigger for the alarm system, although it could equally well be daffodils coming into bloom, or hay being made in the fields, or any other regular annual event which was happening at the time the person died. Therefore, if you associate losing someone with a particular date, the next time that date comes round, or is mentioned, the alarm system throws in a danger warning.

The laid-back person will ask themselves what the problem is, will recall that this was the day so-and-so died, will recall the person probably with a degree of fondness, and will get on with what they were doing anyway. The next time the date comes up they may still remember the person who died but it will be a positive memory.

The person with the quick-acting arousal, however, will be reminded of what happened and will then start to recall how bad it made them feel! In doing this, they are telling the alarm system to just keep on bringing all those negative memories and feelings to the fore.

As we have already seen, whenever we experience negative feelings in any situation or circumstance, the alarm system does its best to register all the apparently connected details so it can give advance warning of potential danger should any of them reappear. The alarm system is not a very sophisticated mechanism and the rules it works by are very basic. As far as it's concerned, anything that was recorded as being present when the negative feeling occurred, could be guilty of causing it.

So, someone you cared about died. You not unnaturally became very upset (negative emotion). The alarm system noted both this negative emotion as well as everything else that was going on at the time. This may have been the date, events in nature, or even the boiled egg you were eating when you heard the sad news.

You would then go through a grieving process and emerge at the other side. But then some months later you might notice that you were reluctant to eat boiled eggs, or that you had some degree of dread about that date on the calendar as it came close again. To have such 'warnings' from the alarm system is normal and shows it is doing the job it was designed to do.

Where we need to make changes is in the way we react to the warnings it gives.

Of course, not everyone falls into the category of being either laid-back or of having a very quick-acting arousal system. There are degrees between, just as we aren't all either six foot or four foot tall.

Where the laid-back person scores is that although they get the warnings, they step back and ask why the warning is being given. This then enables them to react to it in a more helpful way, such as recalling something positive about the person who died rather than just re-experiencing their own negative emotions at the time.

In some situations it is more helpful to simply note why a warning happens and then not even think about it again if doing so serves no positive purpose. This could apply to those times when we remember making fools of ourselves or doing something we regret. If you can't learn anything further from re-visiting a memory, why go there simply in order to make yourself feel bad?

In reality what happens is that we keep going over events like this in our minds in all their horror. We keep reminding ourselves how bad it was, how stupid we were.

This happens a lot with people who are suffering with depression. They spend their days doing less and less and thinking more and more. Their thoughts return to their worries or past negative events. This in turn keeps the depression going.

This is why mindfulness can help to reduce repeated episodes of depression. It teaches awareness of thoughts and feelings as they happen. It teaches us to keep our thoughts in the present moment and wean them away from all those negatives which are past or which may never happen.

***

The Two Monks and the Beautiful Girl

This story is about two monks, a wise old master and a young novice, who were journeying to a distant monastery. They walked side by side, mainly in silence, each mindful of the moment and what it contained—the sound of the birds, the breeze on their skin, the gentle warmth of the sun, the movement in their own bodies as they travelled . . .

After a couple of hours they reached a stream which was flowing rapidly, swollen with melting snow from the mountains. On the bank of the stream was a beautiful girl

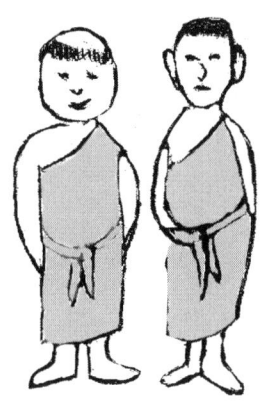

wearing shorts and a T-shirt. She saw the two men approaching and ran up to them in distress.

"Please, please can you help me?" she entreated. "I have to get across this stream, but I can't swim and it's flowing too fast for me!"

The young monk turned to the older monk. "Master," he began, "what are we to do, for we are forbidden to associate with women?"

To his horror, the older monk shrugged, turned to the girl and said, "Jump on my back."

The girl did as she was told and the two monks waded across the stream. When they reached the other side, the older monk put the girl down on the grass. She thanked him profusely and then they went their separate ways. After several more hours the younger monk stopped in his tracks.

"Master," he said, "I cannot keep quiet any longer. I'm very concerned."

"About what are you so concerned?" asked the master.

"About that girl," he spluttered.

"Which girl would that be?" enquired the older monk, puzzled.

"You know . . . that one you carried across the stream . . ."

"Ah, her," the older monk nodded as he began to walk on. *"I left her back there on the bank many hours ago and you should have done the same."*

***

Action Points

1. Monitor your own alarm system warnings. Notice all those everyday instances when you feel mildly anxious or worried and pause to consider why you are feeling that. Then consider what, if anything, you could usefully be doing about it. If there's nothing you can do at this point in time, re-focus instead on something here and now.

2. Keep practising the meditations because these teach the basic skill of being in the moment, of being aware of what we are experiencing here and now. It doesn't matter whether you focus on touch or sound at this stage. Keep meditating for thirty seconds or so at odd moments throughout the day.

***

Test Yourself

1. What is the one and only thing which any one of us truly has the power to control?

2. What is resistance?

3. By what means can we change the way we feel about things which have happened to us?

10 – Meditating on Your Breath

This meditation is the one which is usually taught first. I stopped doing this in our courses as we have many participants who either have asthma or suffer from panic attacks. Sufferers with either of these conditions tend to have associated anxiety with their breathing and so find it almost impossible to allow themselves to just accept their breath and observe it, as is required for this lesson. Therefore we teach focus on touch and sound in the first instance.

Those reluctant to focus on their breath by the third lesson are then invited to just do their own thing during the meditation and focus on touch or sound instead. Generally by the end of the course those same participants are sufficiently adept at keeping a mindful focus to be able to focus on their breath as well without any distress.

So if you are someone who finds focusing on breath uncomfortable for any reason, I suggest you simply listen to the 'Breath' meditation track to familiarize yourself with what's involved. Then you might from time to time when you are feeling calm, see if you are able to focus on just one breath.

Once you are able to focus on a single breath without anxiety, you will be able to increase it to two . . . and so on.

The beauty of meditating on your breath is that you can do it anywhere at any time and nobody would even know. As explained on the download, it is simply a matter of observing what your breath feels like as you breathe normally, and of keeping your attention on just your breath, as it enters your body, where it goes, and as it leaves again.

You don't pass judgment on how you're breathing, whether you're doing it right, etc. because whatever you are doing is just fine. Meditating on breath is about observing it and accepting it just as it is.

11 – Do We Always Need To Have an Opinion?

These days everyone appears to think they must have an opinion about everything, even those things which have no relevance to their lives whatsoever. We even have to give opinions about everyday things we might not have given headspace to previously. How many "How was it for you?" surveys have you been asked to complete recently? That is now the way of the western world.

TV soaps are full of characters who don't know the meaning of minding their own business and create havoc as a result. Ok, I realise that it wouldn't make compulsive viewing if everyone lived mindfully, but the problem is that viewers then take what they watch as an example of how they should live.

There is a tendency in our society for us to feel we have to pass judgment on absolutely everything, even when it doesn't concern us. The media focus on the down-side of events in their news bulletins just so we can have even more bad vibes. We are made to believe that we should have an opinion about everything. Do we really need one?

This brings us to the third component of mindfulness which is non-judgment.

Many people in the groups I run become confused as to the difference between acceptance and non-judgment. The difference is only a slight shift in focus. Acceptance may follow judgment.

To accept something you have to be aware of what it is and then choose not to resist it. The example of this which I quoted previously was of doing the ironing. Most people tell me that they hate ironing. Many get around this by not doing any and either wearing creased clothes, drying them in a tumble drier, or getting someone else to do their ironing.

If, on the other hand, none of these options is available and they find themselves having to iron some items, they will typically perform the task whilst telling themselves how much they hate and resent it. They will probably also have very tense body posture throughout.

Acceptance would say that if you are stuck with having to do something, then why resist and give yourself negative vibes? Far better to focus mindfully on what you are doing by having maybe an awareness of the relaxed movements of your body as you iron, or by simply watching the creases as they get smoothed away.

In other words you do just what you have been doing in the meditations—you focus your awareness on sensory input of some kind. This could be the fresh smell of the clothes or the sensation of the iron gliding over the fabric. You refrain from thinking in words at all.

Judgment, on the other hand, happens when you mentally comment on the goodness or badness of something. So, in the example above, you may have thought, "I've got to do the ironing tonight. I hate ironing!" The second part of that thought, "I hate ironing" is a judgment.

Most of the time we habitually make judgments which serve no purpose other than to make us feel bad. If you know you must do some ironing tonight, what do you gain by then reminding yourself how much you hate doing it?

Take another example. You go to see your GP because you have sprained your ankle. You are asked to take a seat in the waiting room. All the chairs are identical. You find a vacant chair and sit down. There is now no point whatsoever in telling yourself how uncomfortable the chair is because all the others are the same and its either that chair or stand up.

Your injured ankle makes it painful to stand for long periods so this would be a pointless negative judgment. Unless there are positive thoughts you can fill your head with in the meantime, far better to focus instead on a meditation exercise, such as your breath, until your name is called.

Most of us pass numerous negative judgments many times each day, often without even noticing. My great aunt used to do it with the weather. Each day she would comment on it but always negatively. If it was sunny, it was too hot. If there was a breeze it was too 'blowy'. If there was no wind it was too close, etc.

Ok, you may be thinking, but so what? Well each time we pass an unnecessary negative judgment we give ourselves a small charge of negative feeling. If you add up all these tiny negative charges you can become down, or even depressed. (You allow the water to drain from your calm reservoir—see page 20) People who suffer with depression do tend to pass negative judgments more often than others. When they are in a depressive state, this tends to help keep them there.

This is one reason why mindfulness has been shown to reduce the likelihood of relapse in those who suffer depressive episodes. It encourages them to become aware of, and change, their thinking habits and so reduce these constant and unnecessary negative vibes. Our thoughts are part of us just as much as our skin, bones, blood etc. We can change what happens to our physical bodies by changing our thoughts.

In order to pass a judgment on something we have to think. Most of our thinking is done using words. As I write this I am thinking what to write next. My thoughts are in the form of words in my head. If I were unable to use language, my thinking would be far less complex.

Can you recall what you used to think about when you were a small baby, before you learnt to talk? Probably not. Some people can recall images of moments when they were babies, but little more than that.

I can recall lying in my pram under a tree at the bottom of our garden, watching the leaves move. No doubt this happened to me every day when I was put in my pram in the garden to sleep so it's little wonder that an image of what I could see has lodged in my memory. But it's nothing more than an image. There are no feelings or thoughts associated with it.

The Abuse of Language

Many people have no recollection whatsoever of events at a very young age. It is only once we learn language that our memories become more complex. It is only when we become proficient with language that we think complex thoughts about things other than what is happening in the here and now.

It's by using language in our heads that we cause ourselves most of our problems. It's thinking in words which allows us to bring memories of past happenings into the here and now. It's thinking in words which allows us to worry about what might happen in the future.

When we are looking forward to something nice, or good, or exciting, the power of thought is a positive thing. When we remember events and experiences which make us feel happy, thought is beneficial.

Unfortunately, we all too often use this same power to remind ourselves of things which didn't go well, which upset us, or caused us anxiety, or to imagine what might happen in the future if things go wrong.

Sometimes it is perfectly justified to think about the future. If we need to plan something, write a shopping list, or work out the monthly budget the ability to use out heads is useful. But many of us don't simply restrict such thinking to planning with a purpose. Most of us are in the habit of visualising what might happen if the worst were to happen. In doing so we make ourselves feel bad.

At other times we dwell on past 'failures'—times when we failed to be perfect (in our eyes). We beat ourselves up about this, and even indulge in feeling guilty.

When is judgment justified?

A judgment would be justified, for example, if you were in a furniture shop to buy a new dining table and chairs for the home. In this case there would be a very good reason to consider how comfortable each chair was when you sat on it. In fact it would be very stupid under such circumstances not to pass judgment.

Judgment is valid if you have to make a decision about something.

Judgment is also ok when it's positive and so makes you feel good to think it.

If you sit in the GP's waiting room and think that the chair is the most comfortable you've ever sat on and can focus on the feeling of comfort and pleasure at sitting there, then that's fine. Each positive thought we have is very good for us since it enhances our positive experience and is therefore well worth having.

Another valid time for judgment is if you're aiming to improve your performance at something. You then judge what you've done with a view to finding ways to improve the next time and you focus on what went well, rather than getting bogged down in what went wrong.

It's ok to have thoughts when you're working something out. But the majority of our daily thoughts are unnecessary judgments, even about ourselves. We constantly judge our own performances and if these are negative judgments, all we succeed in doing is making it less likely we'll do better the next time.

If you are plagued by thoughts of how badly you did it the last time, your next performance is very likely to repeat it again.

Imagine you are a snooker player who missed a vital corner shot in their last big game and so lost out on winning a championship. If you are prone to negative judgments, you might have repeatedly replayed that fatal poor shot in your mind. The next time you come to play a similar shot your brain will recognize the situation and give you a warning reminder because this memory is linked to past negative emotion. Even if you hadn't remembered that incident, you do now!

So you become anxious and start telling yourself, "I mustn't miss the corner pocket like last time . . ." If you do that I guarantee you'll miss it again!

What you've been doing is training yourself to repeat that missed shot by going over it again and again in your mind. Then when you came to play the shot, your brain gives you exactly what you have been rehearsing—a poor shot.

The brain doesn't understand "don't" or "mustn't". What it hears is "must" or "do". So whenever we tell ourselves what we mustn't do, we are in fact making sure that we do it! (more about this later)

If you want to rehearse the shot in your mind (and there is evidence that you can do this almost as effectively as doing it for real) then you must imagine yourself doing it perfectly. Picture yourself succeeding, and you're stacking the odds in your favour.

By all means evaluate a performance to find out where it could be improved, but then move on and focus on the improvements and not on what went wrong last time!

Suppose you're learning to dance salsa and in class your teacher mentions that upper body tension is spoiling your dancing. If the teacher is a good one they will put it in such a way that the focus is on what you need to do to improve and they will at the same time encourage you with some positive comments as well.

When you dance you now need to be mindful of that upper body tension and release it as you have been instructed whenever you notice it. You pass judgment on yourself when you successfully feel it's improved—positive judgment. In using positive judgment you are always thinking about how you want it to be i.e. the improvement. You are not constantly thinking about how it is when it's wrong.

Judgment is ok when it's focusing on positive progress.

On the whole we each do the best we're capable of at a particular moment at any time, given the circumstances in that moment. Therefore, even if we judge it afterwards to be not good enough, it was the best we could do at that time under those conditions.

People rarely deliberately do less than their best on any occasion. Maybe their best proves to be insufficient for the task in hand, but provided it was their best at that time then they couldn't have done more. The media are particularly adept at criticising the performance of sports teams and stage performers. Many sportsmen, singers and actors say that they never read reviews—a very wise decision.

***

The next story is quite short.

Working harder and harder

A meditation student went to his teacher and asked, "If I practise every day, how long will it take me to become a Master of the art?"

"Ten years", said the teacher.

"But what if I work really hard at it," persisted the student, "how long?"

"Twenty years."

The student was puzzled. "But what if I work really, really hard and try my very best. How long then?"

The teacher shook his head. "Thirty years," he said.

"But I just don't understand!" protested the student. "Every time I say I'll try even harder, you're telling me it will take longer and longer. Why?"

"Well," said the teacher softly, "because when you have one eye on the goal, you only have one eye on the path."

Struggle of any kind is a negative emotion.

***

Action Points

As an exercise, note how many unnecessary judgments you pass in the course of the average day. Keep a notebook one day and write each one down. Only do this exercise once because you don't want to train yourself in that way of thinking. But until you become aware of them, you can't stop them.

Once aware of these unnecessary judgments, however, you can replace all your previously negative ones with positive ones . After that spend a day mentally noting all the positive judgments you make.

***

Test Yourself

1. What is judgment?

2. When is judgment valid?

12 – What If You've Got It and You Don't Want It?

Imagine someone you live with comes home from work tonight, slumps down in an armchair, puts their hand to their head and says, "I've got a headache." What would most people say to them?

Wouldn't you say something along the lines of, "Have you taken something?" or "Why don't you take an aspirin?'

It's one thing to accept having to do the ironing and finding some positive aspect of the task to focus on instead of your unwillingness to do it. It's a totally different ballgame to be able to accept serious discomfort, such as incurable pain, without feeling any degree of resentment whatsoever. Yet that is what mindfulness would teach.

In our society we appear to have come to expect that if we start to experience anything negative, especially if we don't consider we caused it directly by our own actions, then someone else is responsible in some way and someone will do something about it.

If we have physical pain, we expect the doctor either to cure the cause or at the very least to give us something to take the pain away. If misfortune befalls us we look for someone to blame, someone from whom we can perhaps seek compensation. If we want something such as a holiday or a new car, or even something new to wear, we feel hard done by if we can't go and get it there and then. If we don't have enough money we expect to be able to borrow it.

Because we have these expectations, we also suffer negative emotions when they're not met. Although people vary in the amount of negative emotion such as, pain, disappointment, frustration, loss, etc. which they are able to tolerate, we all try to cope with it by obliterating the discomfort or avoiding it in some way. In other words, we seek to escape it. For some individuals escape takes the form of alcohol, drugs, spending splurges or even comfort eating.

Avoidance in this way is yet another form of resistance.

On the whole I am not suggesting that we put up with negative stuff in our lives. If you have the power to change it, then by all means do so if you decide that's what you want to do. But it's important that you choose to change it and are aware of that.

Changing it also means just that. Changing doesn't mean avoiding or hiding the issue under the carpet. Changing means recognising it for what it is and changing your response to the way you feel about it from negative to neutral at the very least. This is not something which comes naturally to most of us. But it is a skill from which we can all benefit at some time or another

When you go to the dentist, do you spend your time in the chair thinking about what the dentist is doing, wondering why that's being done. Do you find yourself focusing on the discomfort and wishing it would stop soon? I'll bet you do. Why? Don't you trust your dentist?

If the answer to that is, "No," then I suggest you find a dentist whom you do trust. If the answer is, "Yes," then why can't you just let him/her get on with their job? You don't need to lie there concentrating on what they're doing. Practise a mindfulness exercise and focus instead on the feel of your body against the chair, a heaviness and looseness in your muscles, or even just allow your thoughts to drift away to somewhere or something exotic and exciting . . .

Being mindful means being aware of what you are thinking and feeling, but it doesn't mean having to control it at all times. Being mindful includes recognising when to let go because it doesn't require your active attention at that time.

If you've never practised the skill of accepting negatives when they don't really matter you stand no chance of being able to do it when they do. Mindfulness is a skill which requires practice. Therefore, on the course we do a meditation which I call 'Twinges'.

This introduces participants in a light-hearted way to the idea of accepting negatives. The meditation is available as a download. Once you've played it and understood what it's about, I suggest that you try to remember to do it once in a while when you have an itchy nose or some similar minor discomfort, just to keep the skill alive because you never know when an occasion may arise when you'll have to do it for real. I have successfully taught this as a technique to use during childbirth for example.

If you are experiencing something negative which you have no power to change, then change your focus. Focus on some positive angle instead.

To use an everyday example, I know several people who say they dislike air travel. They tolerate it because they want to travel abroad on holiday, but they dread the journey. Before they even leave home they have usually spent many moments dreading the flight and imagining things going wrong.

They get on the plane and then start focusing on all the aspects of the journey which they find scary. They watch the doors being closed and remind themselves, in their thoughts, that they can't get out. They concentrate on the sound of the engine and the movement of the plane as it takes off and lands, listening for something amiss. Some people even have too much alcohol in an attempt to shut out their thoughts.

Let us consider air travel from a different angle.

Firstly, once you are on the plane you have absolutely no power to control what happens to it, so why not just accept the fact and leave it to the pilot. Instead of reminding yourself constantly of the fact that you can't get out, etc. why not focus instead on the fact that for the duration of the journey you can just sit and relax. You don't have to do anything at all. You can indulge in reading, or daydreaming, or maybe even sleeping if you can do that in an upright position. Even if there is little space in your seat, focus on what you do have, rather than on what you don't. You might even spend the time looking forward positively to your holiday!

As the plane takes off and lands make a conscious effort to just relax into your seat, let your stomach muscles relax, because keeping them tight will make no difference whatsoever to how the plane responds.

If this is you, try it. The first time it may not come easily because you will have to overcome all those old past scripts which are telling you to be scared, and which try to make you focus on what could go wrong.

But in time, if you teach yourself to think those positive scripts when considering air travel rather than the old negative ones, your entire experience will change for the better. Each time you catch yourself having one of those old negative thoughts, let it go and replace it with a positive one.

In the days before you travel do this. Whenever the dreaded thought of the flight enters your head, instead of training your brain to see it as something bad, move your mind to something positive about the holiday instead. Brains are creatures of habit. If you keep responding to a negative trigger with a positive thought or visualisation, that trigger will eventually lose its negative charge.

The same applies to other fears such as that of lifts, or of spiders, where there is no real risk involved. Notice the automatic thoughts you allow yourself to have when confronted with what it is that you fear and gradually change your focus. Start with what you have, rather than wishing things were different (acceptance) and then allow yourself to become aware of the positive aspects of that.

The following story demonstrates our habit of failing to truly appreciate what we do have and focusing instead on what we don't have but think we would prefer. Yet when we do this we tend to only see the positives of what it is we think we want. We usually fail to notice the negatives. If we did, we might realise that what we already have is preferable.

***

The Stonecutter

Once upon a time there lived a stonecutter. He wasn't wealthy, but he had enough for his daily needs. He was content with his life in his small cottage with his wife and children, doing a job which gave him satisfaction, and living among neighbours who were also friends.

One day he was asked to repair a wall in the garden of a wealthy merchant. The stonecutter arrived with his hammer and chisels and was astounded at the opulence of the merchant's house which he glimpsed through the main door.

As he worked on the wall he watched many important visitors come and go and began to wish that he too could be wealthy and important like the merchant. And then to his surprise he became the merchant and knew more wealth than he had ever dreamed possible, but others were jealous and envied him.

One day a prince visited the town, escorted by many soldiers, and everyone, no matter how wealthy, had to bow low before him. "How powerful that prince is," the merchant thought. "I wish I could be that prince." And so he became the prince, but he always had to be on his guard that other jealous people didn't harm him.

One day whilst the prince was visiting some of his lands, he felt the sun beating down on him forcing him to remove his robe. "How powerful is the sun," he thought. "I wish I were the sun." And then he became the sun. He shone down on everything and scorched the fields so the people despised him.

But then he found that his power was blocked by something that had moved between him and the earth . . . a large black cloud. "How powerful is that cloud," he thought. "I wish I were that cloud." And so he became the cloud and rained on all below, who cursed him for flooding their fields and villages.

But soon something was pushing him aside and he realised that it was the wind. "How powerful is the wind," he thought. "I wish I could be the wind." And again his wish was granted and he was the wind. He roared through the villages uprooting trees and blowing roofs off homes and was hated by everyone.

But then he came up against something which would not move out of his path no matter how hard he blew ... A big towering rock! "How powerful to be a rock," he thought. "I wish I could be a rock!"

And so he stood there, a huge, solid rock, more powerful than anything on earth. But as he stood there, he heard a tapping sound and felt himself being changed. "What is more *powerful than I, the rock?" he thundered.*

Then he looked down . . . and far below him saw the figure of the stonecutter.

***

Action Point

List some of the things in your life which you tend to see in negative terms—these may be current situations or past events. Shift your focus to the positive and see what else you can find in them. There is a positive angle to everything, you just have to look for it.

13 – Twinges Meditation

This meditation is designed to introduce you to the possibility of accepting something negative which you are unable to change. This may be a negative emotion, such as depression, bereavement or even frustration, or a negative feeling such as pain (link to download at end of book).

All the meditations I am describing in this book are best practised and learnt when the issues involved aren't important and are ones which you have no undue anxieties about at this time. Once you have mastered the techniques you will be more likely to be able to apply them in circumstances where you are generally less relaxed and when it matters more that you stay in control.

In order to practise mindful acceptance of a negative sensation, in the course of this meditation track I will suggest that you have an itch on your nose. As we are all aware, once someone suggests you have an itch like that you tend to have one! During this meditation, however, you are asked not to scratch the itch but to simply place your focus on it and observe it for what it is, without wishing it would go away.

Usually, when a participant genuinely focuses on an itch, or twinge, without judgment of any kind, the twinge either moves elsewhere or disappears.

Some years ago a lady who experienced panic attacks was attending the group sessions. One of her main fears was of travelling on dual carriageways because she thought that should she panic she would be unable to turn off. She could not drive herself and always travelled as a passenger.

Just after doing the session about twinges, she was travelling somewhere on a dual carriageway and noticed that she was starting to feel sick. This time, however, instead of battling with and resisting the sick feeling, she remembered the twinges meditation and focused on the queasy feeling by simply observing it and not judging. She reported that, soon after she started doing this, the sick feeling moved from her stomach to her left arm. In her left arm it wasn't a problem and so she was able to let it go. (I don't know how feeling sick in your left arm feels but those were her very words.)

If you are able to notice when you develop an itch or similar in everyday life after you have learnt this technique and can allow yourself to repeat the exercise of just observing and accepting it rather than scratching to relieve it, this will prove useful should you ever need to use it for real. It is, however, very hard to remember to notice because our usual habit is to feel an itch and just scratch it without giving it a second thought.

You may become aware of other instances of mild discomfort during which you can practise.

14 – If You Don't Want It, Why Think About It?

We looked previously at the consequences of remembering a past failure and focusing on it. This tends to cause us to repeat the failure. Although we all instinctively do it due to the nature of our survival instincts, there is no real need to constantly focus on what we don't want.

Cheryl wanted to lose weight. In order to help her focus on her goals I asked her why she wanted to lose weight because people's reasons differ greatly.

For example, some people want to lose weight because they believe it will make them appear more attractive to someone. Others wish to be lighter so they don't get breathless walking upstairs. Some may wish to fit into a particular outfit they used to wear. Whatever the reasons for wanting to lose weight, you always stand a far better chance of success if you frame your goals in positive terms.

Cheryl answered my question saying that she didn't want to feel breathless when she went dancing. Furthermore, she wanted to get rid of excess flab around her middle.

I then pointed out that she had given me reasons for wanting to lose weight in negative terms. Her reasons were all things she wished to avoid. Why focus on the negative?

ACTION POINT:

Momentarily picture something in your mind, anything at all . . . but **don't** *imagine a pink elephant . . .*

***

What happened? I'll bet that you did picture a pink elephant however briefly. In order for your mind to register what not to imagine, it first has to identify it.

Those things which spend most time in your thoughts, are those things which are most likely to come into being. So if you spend your time focusing on what you don't want, you're effectively drawing it to you!

EXPERIENTIAL EXERCISES - TRY ONE OR BOTH

OPTION ONE

1. Find something in the kitchen drawer or workshop that has a central hole through which you can tie some string— bottle openers are good, or a large metal nut.

2. Get a length of thin cord or string about 1metre long and tie the bottle opener on one end of it.

3. Now you suspend the bottle opener by holding the other end of the string. It should hang vertically. We are trying to create a plumb line effect. (If you have a plumb line used for wallpaper hanging that is ideal for this).

4. Place a CD on the floor, preferably one which you don't value, a dud one or similar.

5. Give the string with the weight on the end to a friend or family member. Tell them to hold their arm out straight in front of them, holding the end of the string and centering the weight over the hole in the centre of the CD.

6. Now they must do their best to keep the weight suspended above the hole. As they do so in their mind they must repeatedly say to themselves, "This mustn't swing from side to side". It's very important that they think that thought and nothing else. As they do it keep telling them, "It mustn't swing from side to side."

OPTION TWO

1. Place a wastepaper bin some ten feet away.

2. Screw up a few sheets of paper into balls.

3. Ask a friend to throw the balls of paper so they land as close to the bin as possible but they must NOT actually land inside the bin. As they throw the friend must think, "It mustn't go in the bin." As the person throws keep reminding them, "It mustn't go in the bin."

If you do the pendulum exercise you will probably find that it does swing from side to side and if you throw paper at the bin you will find that most of them do land inside the bin. You get what you think about. The brain disregards the 'not' in 'do not' or 'don't' and interprets it as 'do'.

You might then repeat each exercise but this time with positive reinforcement such as, "Make sure it hangs over the central hole", or "Make sure it lands outside the bin". If the person hasn't been cheating (and having their own thoughts rather than thinking what they were told) there will be fewer errors the second time around because the focus is then on what must be achieved, rather than on what mustn't.

If you have goals they must be worded in positive terms.

We reframed Cheryl's goals to read:

I want to be able to dance energetically like I used to.

I want a slim streamlined midriff.

It's not only negative instructions which draw us away from our goals. Unnecessary negative judgments also drip feed a sense of negativity into us and promote stress.

***

ACTION POINT:

Answer the following question:

If you knew 100% that you couldn't fail, what would you do?

....

***

What holds many of us back from doing what we truly in our hearts wish to do is fear of failure in one way or another.

As the story at the end of Chapter 11, Working Harder and Harder, pointed out, it is the journey we are aware of if we are mindful and stay in the moment, not the goal. If we fear failure we are focusing on a point in the future. In which case we are not making the most of now. If what we do now eventually leads us to the goal, then so be it. If it leads somewhere else than that's ok too because the journey will have been worthwhile.

Why do we behave as if there is an eleventh commandment, "Thou shalt not make a mistake"? If a person could get through their entire life without making any mistakes whatsoever, they'd have wasted their time. We learn from our mistakes. Think of all the spectacular mistakes you've made and what they taught you.

Nobody deliberately sets out to make a mistake because if they did, it wouldn't be a mistake. By definition a mistake is something you do wrong without meaning to.

Therefore if we happen to make one, it isn't intended.

This fear of getting it wrong is most probably a hangover from school days when we were told off for making mistakes. Things we learn in childhood tend to root themselves deeply. Those old scripts keep getting replayed long after they stop being relevant. Developing awareness of this gives us the opportunity to change it.

Life is an adventure. Nobody will get through it without mistakes, or, more correctly, learning opportunities. And why should they? As long as you make a point of learning from these, they have been positive experiences. Yet how often do we dwell on what went wrong and beat ourselves up about it, replaying the negative points over and over? Develop awareness of when you do that, catch yourself in the act, and reframe your thoughts around what the positive part of the experience was.

There is another belief which is deeply rooted in many of us from schooldays and one which we are not usually aware of until it's pointed out. I call it 'the path to paradise'.

We believe that if we are careful and good, that our life will gradually follow an upward path, getting better and better, until finally we reach a plateau where everything is just as we want it. At this point we can start to live the life we've dreamed of. This belief is promoted at school where we're told that if we're good and work hard we'll pass exams and get good jobs etc. This is not the case.

Apart from those instances when we know things have gone wrong through our own fault entirely—for example if you had a job as a driver but lost your licence through drink driving—life for everyone has its ups and down. These can happen through no fault of our own, no matter how clever, how rich or poor, powerful or not. But most of us don't behave as if that is the case.

When a downturn hits us we begin to feel powerless. We have been believing the 'path to paradise' myth and so when things go wrong, and it wasn't our fault, we suddenly lose faith in our own ability to keep ourselves from harm. We then focus on how bad things are, wondering why it happened to us.

Because we are in a negative frame of mind we notice every other possible negative in our world. We stop noticing the positives because these don't fit with the pattern. Very often this sort of thinking can lead to depression. Basically we are resisting the downturn. If we accepted it we would just acknowledge its existence and focus on the moment and anything positive found there.

Peter was a very careful, conscientious man. On leaving school he got a job with a major bank. For the next sixteen years he worked hard and climbed the promotion ladder. Then one day his manager called him into the office and said he'd been offered a job with another bank. He invited Peter to go there with him as his deputy.

Peter thought long and hard about this but in the end he decided that it wouldn't look too good on his CV in the future if he'd only ever worked for one employer, so he accepted the offer and moved jobs with his manager. He'd only been in the new job for about six months when the bank announced massive redundancies.

Peter himself wasn't to be made redundant but it was part of his new role to do that to others. Peter was shell-shocked. He found himself thinking that he could've lost his job and since he was new to that bank he'd not have received any redundancy pay, whereas at his former bank he'd accumulated sixteen years' worth.

Even though this hadn't actually happened, Peter became depressed as a result and was then off work for several months.

Peter was a victim of his unshakeable belief in the 'path to paradise'. Had he been mindful he'd have accepted the situation for what it was at that time, because he had no power to change what had happened. He'd have focused instead on positive aspects of the situation and on what he might learn from it and lived in present reality rather than in the 'what might have been'.

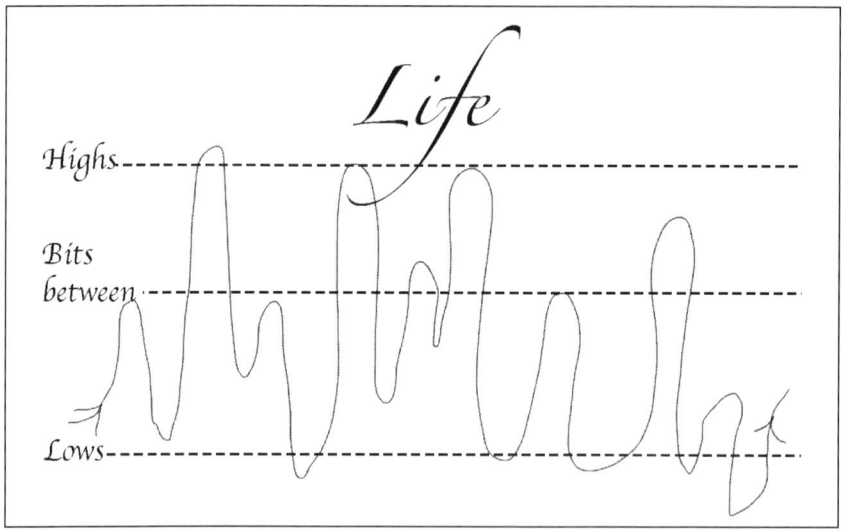

Everyone's life does what the diagram shows although not necessarily in that order. Apart from those things which happen through our own efforts, life throws things at us seemingly at random no matter how powerful or famous we may be.

When we are experiencing a high/good patch, however, how many of us tend to get jumpy? We are almost afraid to enjoy it because we know it won't last.

Well it won't last, nothing is for ever. But we may as well enjoy it while we have it.

And then our fortunes change and a downturn comes. This is often, like the upturn, through no direct fault of our own. This time, however, we embrace it fully. We allow ourselves to believe it's permanent.

But downturns don't last for ever either unless we make a determined effort to hang onto them rather than trying to learn something from them.

***

There's an ancient folk tale which warns against this type of thinking.

I Don't Believe It!

A poor man was working in the forest one day cutting timber. It was hot and he began to feel thirsty. "I wish I had a drink," he thought.

As he did this a cup of cool water appeared in his hand. For a moment the man was stunned, but then he felt very grateful and drank the water. Now he was no longer thirsty, he realised that the hard work was making him hungry. "I wish I had something to eat," he thought.

As he did so, a wonderful meal appeared laid out on a small table before him. Again the man marvelled at this and with thanks he sat down and enjoyed the food.

When he'd eaten he returned to his work but the events had set him thinking. "I seem to be getting my wishes granted," he thought. So he decided to put his new powers to the test.

He wished for a beautiful home. No sooner had he wished than a home beyond his wildest dreams appeared before him. So he then wished for servants to care for the home, and the servants appeared. Then the man wished for a beautiful woman with whom to share this good fortune. The woman stood beside him.

The man looked at the woman and then said to her, "Wait a minute, I must be dreaming all this. This can't happen to me!"

No sooner had he spoken than everything disappeared and he was left alone in the forest with his axe. He looked around and shook his head.

"I knew it was too good to be true." And he went on with his work.

***

Few of us are sufficiently grateful for the good things we have and we constantly dwell on the bad things and the lack.

Action Point

Make a list of all the things in your life for which you have reason to be grateful and allow yourself to be glad you have them.

15 – A Dirty Word You May Not Know

There's a six-letter dirty word in the English language which we all use all the time . . .

Should

Whenever we use the word 'should' we are wishing things were different rather than accepting what is and working with that. We are effectively putting ourselves in a place of powerlessness.

Imagine I'm sitting at my desk. The office door flies open and a man storms in. He approaches the desk, rants and raves at me for a couple of minutes then turns and slams back out. What do I do?

The reaction of many people would be to sit there, steam coming out of their ears, and think things like, "How dare he? He shouldn't have done that!"

But he did do it. What am I going to do about it? I need to look at my real choices—those options which are within *my* power.

The first of my real choices might be to follow him out and shout at him. This is within my power to do if I wanted to.

A second choice might be to report him. This is also within my power. What isn't in my power, however, is what happens to him after I've reported him.

A third option would be to shrug and decide he's not worth reacting to and choose to continue with what I was doing before I was interrupted.

From a power point of view it wouldn't matter which of those three options I chose because they are all within my power to put into practice. The one which is not in my power is wishing it hadn't happened which is what I'm doing when I just sit thinking, "How dare he? He shouldn't have done it!"

Whenever you catch yourself thinking or saying 'should' ask yourself what your real options are instead. In this life there are things you have to do, things you want to do, but there are no things you should do.

If you don't want to do it, and you don't have to do it, don't do it!

Now you might be thinking that if you only ever did what you wanted to do, you'd never do stuff like washing the car or mowing the lawn, or maybe even going to work.

Not so.

Take going to work as an example. Suppose you wake up in the morning and realise it's Monday and think, "Yuk it's work today." The unmindful person would then probably have a head conversation with themselves as to how much they resented going to work and wished they didn't have to go etc. This would simply serve to give them negative feelings but they would go to work anyway because they felt they should.

A mindful person, on the other hand, might catch themselves thinking negatively about having to go to work and turn it around. They would acknowledge that they were choosing to go to work because if they didn't they wouldn't earn money, wouldn't be able to support their loved ones etc.

The difference is that they are now telling themselves that they have chosen to go to work. Although it might be nice not to go to work, that isn't an option today if they want to keep the lifestyle they have.

Remember, we looked previously at the fact that although we always have options, we don't always have the ones we wish we had so we have to choose between the ones available to us. In this example it's no longer a case of you feeling you should go to work but now you can tell yourself you are choosing to go to work. This has a much greater feeling of self-empowerment about it.

Feeling Guilty

We spend time feeling guilty. What about? Usually about things we didn't do which we feel we should have done. Sometimes we feel guilty about things we did but now believe we shouldn't have. See that 'should' word cropping up again and again and indicating that it's all wishful thinking.

Whatever we've done or not done can't be changed so we need to get over it. If you believe you made a mistake you make amends if this is possible. If it's not possible you can only make a mental note to learn from the experience and get on with your life.

To wallow in pointless guilt and self reproach is a cop-out because all the while you're using that guilt as an excuse not to get on with now. Maybe because you're afraid you'll get it wrong or make a mistake. But, as we've already seen, so what?

Now it's not wrong in itself to wallow in self pity or guilt or even feeling down or depressed as long as you are aware that you're doing it, are choosing to do it, and get some positive feedback from doing it. Just don't kid yourself.

Such behaviour becomes damaging when we kid ourselves that we can't help it. As we've already seen when looking at the power of thoughts, if you won't attempt to control yours, nobody else can do it for you.

Life is an adventure, a journey of discovery. The person who's afraid of getting it wrong never gets it at all. It's your life and it's for you to make of it what you wish. You can be whoever you wish to be, but you have to allow yourself to be it.

It's Not Always About You

We are each responsible for doing the best we can with ourselves by being true to ourselves. This means allowing ourselves to do more of those things that feel right for us, developing those skills we have that we are drawn towards.

Unfortunately many of us get waylaid by worrying about what others think of us. We try to be what we or others think we should be rather than focusing on actually being ourselves.

We might feel it necessary to be aware of what's going on in our world, but we can't do anything about much of it. By all means if you feel strongly about a world issue, take whatever steps you feel you must. Maybe you choose to donate money to a cause you believe in. Perhaps you join an action group of some sort. It's for each of us to focus on what most concerns us.

But we can't all take action to right every wrong in the world and so we have to learn to be selective and accept those things we have no power to do anything about at this point in time. Many people become unduly depressed watching TV bulletins about tragedies knowing they can do nothing about them yet feeling they should.

When in need humans are not very different from animals. If you've ever watched a group of horses in a field, you'd notice a pecking order. If they are given some hay, it will be the pushiest who gets first chance to eat it. The horse at the bottom of the pecking order, probably the oldest and least able to stand up for itself, will be lucky to get any at all. People are just the same.

Only when a person's own basic needs are satisfied can they consider those of others and choose to put others first. Think of those scenes on TV news when provisions are delivered to people who've been hit by disaster. When supplies come, people grab what they can for themselves and their families, they don't stand in line and take only their share.

Nature has given us all certain basic instincts in order to ensure the survival of the species. Unless these basic needs are met, a human can't care for another human because their instincts are focusing elsewhere on their own needs. (An exception to this is the care of a parent for its young, which is yet another instinctive drive).

Many therapy books and teachings used to confuse me because they said that you had to love yourself first. As a child I'd been brought up to believe you put yourself last and I could never understand how this 'self first' could be right. But one day the penny dropped.

Unless we feel good about ourselves we are unable to assist others effectively and unselfishly. Therefore, we owe it to ourselves to do the best we can for ourselves because only when we've done that can we be of use to others.

Furthermore, if you aren't prepared to do the best you can with the life you've been given, why would anyone else bother to make you?

Do We Need To Worry What Others Think?

Many of us waste too much energy worrying what others think of us. We frequently misinterpret the reasons why others express negative feelings or behaviour towards us.

I often have clients say to me that they want to be liked. So afraid are they of displeasing anyone at all that they allow themselves to be walked all over by relatives and even so-called friends. Then they wonder why everyone is so nasty to them and what they have done to deserve it.

If you are unwilling to displease anyone at all, you will become a doormat for everyone. Furthermore, people don't decide whether or not they like you according to how you are with them. You might be the nicest, sweetest most generous person in the world, but someone will despise you simply because they are jealous of you.

Generally we don't have negative feelings towards other people because of something they've done or said to us. We have negative feelings because we feel threatened by them in some way. This doesn't have to be a threat of physical violence. It's often because they have something we wish we had—a better house, figure, car, etc. Or maybe they've got away with something that we didn't. Whatever it is, it's about something in our perception of them, not about something which they've done.

So be the person you wish to be. That way you will draw to you those people who will get on with you and repel those who won't. Who wants to spend their time among people who have a totally different outlook on life from them?

If, for example, you always vote Labour, you're not likely to go and join the Conservative party. If you support Everton, you're not likely to choose to spend your leisure hours in a Liverpool supporters' pub.

This approach is tough. Many of us like to shift the responsibility to someone or something else. There are too many, "Yes, buts . . ." But the bottom line is that each one of us is responsible for our own thinking.

Getting in Touch with Now

When I was a child I used to marvel at some neighbours of ours who would go away for two weeks each summer to stay in a lone caravan on a farm somewhere and wouldn't even have a clock with them, let alone any radio or TV. They would get up when it felt right and go to bed when they were tired at the end of the day.

I had a similar experience when sailing a small yacht across the Atlantic. We had no contact with the outside world whatsoever as even the radio had failed. But for those three weeks it felt as if the world had stopped. Every moment was a 'now' moment.

We focused on the present because nothing else was relevant. Even in the gales we just concentrated on what was necessary moment by moment. There was no time to worry about what might happen if . . . When it was calm there was nothing to see but miles of empty ocean and occasional whales, sharks, dolphins, and flying fish. It was bliss.

You may not be able to go anywhere exotic, but it is still possible to give yourself a holiday at home. You could try it for just one day to begin with. Have a day off. Turn off the phones, TV, radio. Don't answer the door and just be. Focus on the moment and do what feels good to you.

Mindfulness says, accept what comes, go with the flow and avoid negative judgments because each one drains away the good vibes. In time everything changes, nothing stays the same.

***

It Will Pass

A student went to his meditation teacher and said, "My meditation is just horrible! I keep getting distracted, I can't focus, it's just horrible!"

"It will pass," said the teacher.

A week later the student went back to his teacher. "My meditation is fantastic. I can meditate for hours without becoming distracted. It's just wonderful!"

"It will pass," said the teacher.

***

Test Yourself

Fill in the blanks, "There are things you .... to do, there are things you .... to do, but there are no things you .... do."

16 – The Big 'T'

Now we come to what is the most challenging part of mindfulness—becoming aware of thoughts.

If you've been doing the meditation exercises which I've described and/or using the downloads, you will probably have started to notice when you have head conversations. You may not yet be able to divert your attention or have found that, even if you do, it soon returns. But that doesn't matter. It's the awareness of what you're thinking that you need to develop first.

As we saw in the early chapters, it's not so much what happens to us that determines what we regard as our life, but rather how we think about what happens. It's about our point of view. To show you what I mean, let's take an example.

Suppose your neighbour's dog got run over this morning. That is a fact.

Your neighbour may regard this event as sad because it was his dog and he loved it.

You on the other hand may be secretly relieved because the dog used to do its business on your lawn.

So we have one event, but two people feeling completely different about it depending on how they think it affects them.

Our thoughts dictate our feelings, not the other way round.

There is a theory which says that the brain only recognises high and low arousal and varying degrees between. Because we can think, however, we add another dimension to this. We judge our own arousal as some degree of good or bad.

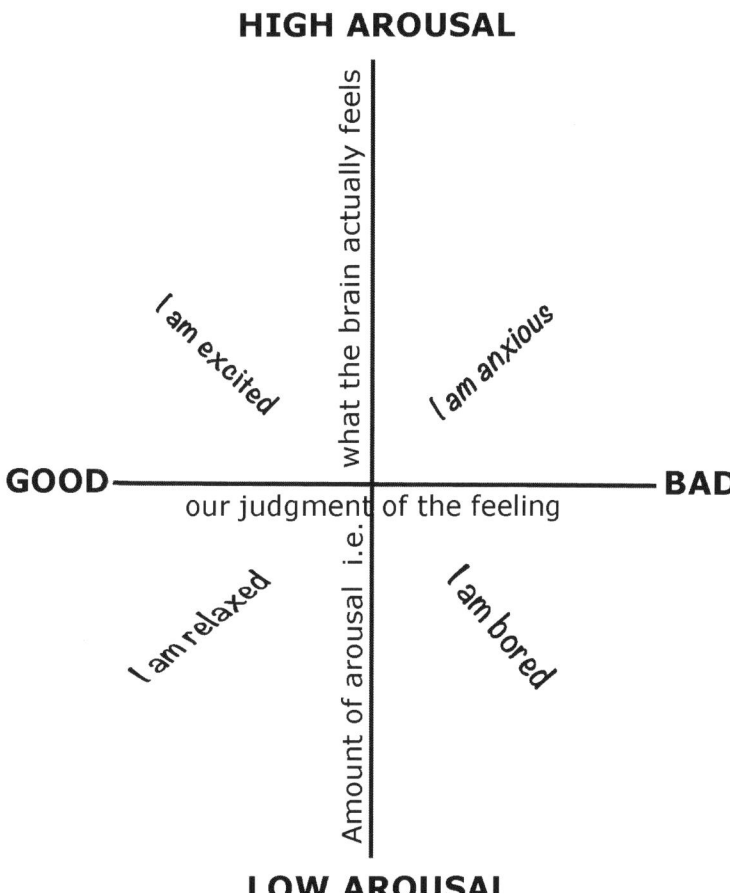

So when we have low arousal and we think its ok, we say we're 'relaxed' . When we have low arousal and we don't want low arousal, we say we're 'bored'. At the other extreme, when we have high arousal and we think its ok, we say we're 'excited'. When we have high arousal and we don't think we should have, we say we're 'anxious'.

But to the brain its simply a case of high or low arousal. Therefore, if we change the label we put on our arousal, we can experience the opposite feeling.

Some years ago I had an experience which demonstrated this principle. I was visiting the Empire State Building in New York with my son. In the building they had a simulator ride. Now I love simulators because they give you all the thrills without the danger.

I'd never go on a real roller coaster for example because I don't trust the cars not to fall off the track. I do, however, like the feeling such a ride gives.

We bought our tickets and took our seats. The fact we had to wear seatbelts was encouraging. We were in the front row. We had no idea what was going to be simulated but that was part of the adventure.

The ride began and the images onscreen were created to make us feel as if we were in a small plane being given a scenic tour of New York City. As the ride continued, the pilot of the plane became more and more manic, doing loop-the-loops and diving down towards the street and up again.

After a while he started to fly along the streets and people could be seen diving to the sides to get out of the way. Then all at once as the plane flew along a street, there was a large truck pulling out of a side street and I just knew that the pilot was going to try and fly under it and that there wouldn't be enough room . . .

At this point I realised that I was gripping the arms of my seat and pushing my feet hard into the floor. As I became aware of this, I thought, "What the hell are you doing, it's only a film!" Then I deliberately released my tight stomach muscles, let go of the arms of the seat and relaxed my body. It felt a bit weird at first but then my emotion changed completely and instead of fear I felt exhilaration and was almost willing the plane to go faster . . .

When it was over as we stood up to leave my son turned to me and said, "Hell, that was embarrassing!

Everyone else was mumbling oooh . . . and aaaagh . . . but you were sitting there cackling!"

I can still remember that exhilaration and continue to try to apply the lesson I learnt. Whenever I catch myself feeling anxious I tell myself there's no point being scared because obviously I can't do anything about it (or I would have). So I mentally label the experience as 'interesting' instead, or I focus on something else entirely—as I suggested when I described a visit to the dentist in an earlier chapter.

What's your first thought when you wake up in the mornings? Is it negative or positive? Do you wake up and think, "Wow another day to be alive!" or do you tend to think, "Oh, no, work again!" or something similar?

If you monitor your thoughts for a few days, you'll be surprised at how big a percentage of those thoughts is negative. We focus on what's wrong rather than on what's right. Much of this is a habit from schooldays when we were constantly told of ways in which we could do better.

Just after I moved house some time back, a friend used to call each Tuesday morning. On her first visit she took a wrong turning and had to ring me on her mobile for directions. On her second visit she was again late as she'd taken another wrong turning and had to double back. As she was leaving on that second occasion she said to me, "I won't take the wrong turning next week." I then pointed out that the brain doesn't do 'not' and that she was effectively telling me that she would take the wrong turning again. What she needed to learn to do was focus on the positives rather than the negatives and say, "I will take the right road next week".

It's the little things like this which add up. Why focus on a negative when you can turn it around?

Another bad habit is what I call the 'chocolate ice cream syndrome.' Suppose I'm eating a piece of treacle tart and custard when somebody brings me a bowl of chocolate ice cream. I see the ice cream and realise that I much prefer that to treacle tart. I don't have to eat all the treacle tart before I can have the ice cream. All I have to do is push the bowl aside and start eating the ice cream instead. The treacle tart still exists but my focus is now on the ice cream.

I'm sure some readers are feeling uncomfortable at this concept. As children we were taught we had to finish what we were doing before we did something else. We maybe had to finish our first course before we had our pudding etc. Maybe as children it was relevant. But now we are grown up and we no longer have to think like children.

You are answerable to yourself first and foremost. You don't necessarily still have to play by the same rules. I'm not saying that we all become totally irresponsible and just do whatever we feel like doing at the moment regardless. What I am saying is that we need to become aware of our own limiting beliefs and question them to discover whether they are actually relevant in those circumstances or not.

We are each responsible for following our own dreams. If you choose not to follow a particular dream because you're scared, then admit that to yourself and stop making excuses—accept who you are. If you're not going to follow a dream then let it go and find one that you are prepared to go for.

Wake up and live your life rather than exist through it. Do the best you possibly can with each moment that comes. What you achieve may or may not be all that you hoped for, but if you did the best you could at the time you accept that and focus forward rather than becoming embroiled in pointless regrets.

Phobias and Mindfulness

The problem with thoughts is that we tend to treat them as if they're important and we must listen to them. Anyone who has a phobia of any sort will confirm this fact.

Strictly speaking a phobia is defined as a fear for which there is no foundation in reality. That's to say the feared thing doesn't actually threaten life, there is no real danger. In most cases what the sufferer really fears is having some sort of panic attack in the presence of the feared object. Therefore, lift phobia is more a fear of being stuck in a lift and having a panic attack whilst there, than a real belief that the lift isn't safe.

The same applies to fear of flying for the most part. If, like me with the roller coaster, you have a genuine belief that the thing in question is unsafe, then nothing will persuade you to even attempt to entrust yourself to it, unless it was truly a matter of life or death.

Suppose you're afraid of lifts. The most common reasons for this fear are either that the lift will crash or, more commonly, that it will break down and you'll be trapped inside and will then panic and be unable to escape. This fear has been built up over time. It may have developed after you were actually trapped in a lift and experienced a panic attack there, or it may just be something which has never actually happened but which you fear might. Let me demonstrate using as an example a lady I knew many years ago.

Jessica was disabled and used a wheelchair. Her mother was admitted to the local teaching hospital and Jessica wanted to visit her. Unable to walk up the stairs, Jessica's only route to the ward was via the lift. Having decided that she really wanted to visit her mother, she then started visualising what would happen. She was actually picturing the worst case scenario—that she went into the lift and panicked between floors!

What was this achieving? As we have already seen, the alarm system learns from what we think as much as from by what actually happens. So she was in fact training herself to do the very thing she feared—to panic in the lift. Therefore, when she actually entered the lift for real, the alarm system recognised the situation as the one she'd imagined so often and started sending her dire warnings. Her panicky feelings then started.

The better way, if she found herself visualising her visit to her mother in advance, Would be to visualise it happening as she'd like it to be i.e. calm and safe. That way she'd at least stand a chance of not receiving a warning from the alarm system the moment the lift doors opened (or even earlier). But even if she had done her homework, she might still have received a warning from the alarm system in the form of a thought such as, "What if I panic?"

All phobia sufferers have these "What if...?" warnings from their alarm systems when they think they may come into contact with the source of their fear. And what do they then do? They listen to that thought as if it's someone in authority tapping them on the shoulder and making them listen! We all need to realise that thoughts are not facts, and to stop behaving as if they are.

This is where mindfulness practice comes in. When you practise being mindful of your thoughts you learn to observe them but not engage with them. You recognise them merely as thoughts which only have power if you hand it to them.

So had Jessica been mindful of her thoughts she would have noted that she had received a warning but she would have chosen not to react to it. If she hadn't reacted to the warning, the panic would not have followed. You have to think about panicking, or about trying to stop panicking, in order for it to take hold.

I'm not saying that those of you reading this who have phobias or panics can simply stop them at the first attempt. You can't. But you can do it with practise and perseverance using the technique of being mindful of your thoughts and letting them go. You have to learn the technique by working on ordinary, non-threatening thoughts and once you have learnt how to do it, you can then apply it to those alarm system warnings.

Another range of situations when people pay heed to thoughts is when being reminded of sad or painful events that have happened in the past. Again, once these memories jump in, we tend to pay full attention to them. Why? All that does is tell the alarm system to keep them coming.

I have a friend who died in tragic circumstances. At first when I visited her grave, memories of how and when she died would jump into my head. By using mindfulness techniques I became aware that this was happening and when those bad memories came I'd simply notice they were there and deliberately recall instead those good times with my friend.

In time, and with some degree of perseverance on my part, I stopped receiving automatic reminders of her death when I went to the cemetery and found all those lovely memories flooding in instead. After all, who wants to be remembered for the way in which they died rather than for all the good times they gave and achievements they had during their life?

***

There is yet another folk tale to tell. This one demonstrates how our thoughts can prevent us from achieving.

The Boastful Archer

In a village lived a young archer who considered himself very skilled. He had won many competitions and had beaten everyone who had challenged him. He could hit a target with his first arrow and then split that arrow with his second shot.

In a neighbouring village lived an old man who had been recognised as a supreme master of the skill of archery in his day. The young archer could not rest until he had defeated the old man in a contest. He continually pestered the old man to take up his challenge.

One day, tired of the young archer's nagging, the old man stood up, collected his bow and arrows and beckoned the young archer to follow him. Curiously the younger man followed the master out of the village and high up into the mountains. Finally they reached a deep chasm spanned only by a flimsy log.

Without hesitation, the master stepped out onto the log, selected a distant tree as his target and fired a direct hit.

Stepping back onto firm ground, he turned to the younger man. "Your turn," he said.

The younger man was unable to move. He stood rooted to the spot, staring in terror at the log and the chasm below.

"Ah," said the master, shaking his head slowly. "You have much skill with your bow. But you have no skill with the mind that fires the shot."

***

Action Point

Experiment with re-labelling your feelings when you encounter something that makes you anxious. Tell yourself it's 'interesting' instead. If you ever find yourself feeling bored, re-label it as 'relaxed'.

If you tend to feel anxious on planes (or in any similar situation such as at the dentist), next time just tell yourself you can't control anything by being anxious. Release your tension and find something to enjoy about the journey instead. If you keep doing this you will eventually change the way you feel about air travel or the dentist, or anything else to which you apply this principle.

17 – What To Do with Thoughts When You Meditate

As with the other meditations the aim is to observe what thoughts come into your head whilst doing the meditation, but then not hang onto them and think about them and not to engage with them.

How often has someone said to you, "You're not listening to me!"

I doubt there is anyone to whom this has not happened at some time. Under those circumstances you are able to hear the sounds of the words being spoken but your mind is not engaging with them so they remain no more than sounds. They only take on a meaning when you react to them in some way.

To meditate on thoughts is to do something similar but his time it is your own head that is speaking to you. A thought has no power whatsoever until we either react to it on auto-pilot (as happens with habits) or we choose to consciously focus on it and engage with what it's saying to us.

It takes a while to get the hang of this because most of us have been in the habit of trying not to think about certain things by either pushing the thought away (usually unsuccessfully) or by swamping it with something else (distraction). As I mentioned earlier, neither of these really works because to push something away or distract yourself from something you have to first focus on it.

When you become aware of a thought during this meditation you are going to choose first to acknowledge awareness of it, then let it pass on by. You do this as follows:

STEPS FOR THOUGHTS MEDITATION

1. Decide on the imagery to visualise for letting the thought go by. The most commonly used examples are

(i) A procession carrying banners and you write the thought on one of the banners

(ii) A train

(iii) Moving clouds

(iv) My own favourite of a small plane trailing a banner behind it. I write the thought on the banner.

(v) A leaf on which you write the thought then toss it into a stream and watch it carried away.

These are just some examples. You may use any image that appeals to you.

2. Follow meditation instructions as usual.

3. When you become aware of having a thought, visualize your chosen scene and imagine yourself writing the thought letter by letter and then seeing that something just move past you, taking the thought with it.

Having to visualize writing each and every letter of the thought, rather than just seeing the whole thing slapped down in one move, has the effect of separating you from what the thought is actually saying. It helps you to see the thought as just words. When a thought is no more than the words which make it up, you can let it go because it has no meaning.

4. You then return to the meditation and carry on until another thought pops into your mind, at which point you repeat the above.

5. Now do the Thoughts Meditation download. You will probably have to practice this one by listening to the download several times in order to get the visualization firmly established in your mind. This isn't really one that you can do just by thinking it yourself in the initial stages.

Once you have got to know your own preferred visualisation and have used this in a few meditations, you can then use the technique to let go of any unwanted thoughts you have during the day. After some practise you will no longer need to actually see the words written when using the technique during daily life, it will be enough to simply see something being carried away in your mind's eye by whatever means you used during the meditations.

Your brain will start to associate your chosen visualization with letting go of whatever thought has entered your head. This is a benefit of the brain's habit of linking things to be helpful for once!

This means that after a while, whenever you catch yourself engaging with an unhelpful thought, you merely have to pause and visualise your chosen scene and your brain will let go of the thought. With practise you will be able to let go of any thoughts you find unhelpful whenever you choose.

The other result is that you will no longer be adding more negative emotion to those negative thoughts when they pop into your head. This means you will no longer be reinforcing them. For that reason your alarm system will start to re-evaluate them and decide you no longer need to be warned about them so will reduce or even stop giving them altogether.

I once used to have panic attacks on the London Underground, when held up on the road because there was an accident, and several other similar situations. Through simply moving my focus elsewhere when such thoughts invaded they finally stopped happening at all. I wasn't aware exactly when such situations stopped triggering thoughts of panic. I just know that I can't make them happen now even if I try to.

So if I return now to Jessica and the lift. All she had to learn to do was to notice when her alarm system was suggesting she might panic and let the thought pass on through, then focus her mind on something more pleasant. I know this works because I overcame my own panic attacks in much the same way, and now I don't even get the "What if . . .?" thoughts in the first place.

This technique can also be applied to people who have a form of obsessive thinking. If this is you, when your head tells you to do something and you choose not to but feel anxious afterwards, let those anxious thoughts get carried away. (The link to the meditation download is at the end of book.)

18 – Where To Now?

I hope that by now you are coming to realise that you can focus on just about anything whilst meditating. The idea of meditation is to just be.

As we have discovered through this book, the three main parts of mindfulness are:

AWARENESS

Being aware of what we are experiencing moment by moment. Allowing our focus to be in the here and now and not wandering off in our heads to things past or things which are yet to come. Although there are some past things which have to be learnt from, and some future details which may need to be planned, once the learning and planning has been done we must let those thoughts go and focus back on now.

There are various sayings which refer to this:

Today is the tomorrow you worried about yesterday

The future will always remain the future

Today is the first day of the rest of your life

NON-JUDGMENT

In our everyday lives we rarely accept non-judgmentally, even when it doesn't concern us. How often do you pass some kind of negative judgment to yourself about what someone else has done or said?

ACCEPTANCE

Knowing when to stop resisting what we have no power to change and choose to just go with the flow instead.

Hopefully by now you have realised that any form of struggle is pointless. Struggle implies tension of some sort. Tension is a negative emotion. Negative emotion drains the calm reservoir.

When you catch yourself struggling with anything take a mindful pause . . .

Ask yourself if you want to be doing it . . . ?

If you do then just relax into it and do the best you can. Struggle never improved anyone's performance.

If you don't want to do it ask yourself if you have to . . . ?

If you think you have to, tell yourself you are choosing to continue with it and get on with it without resisting.

**

Whatever Comes, Whatever Goes Meditation

This is the final meditation download. This involves focusing on nothing in particular, but just noticing what comes into awareness moment by moment and allowing it to pass on through without thinking about it or passing judgment on it.

As with all the meditations, you probably won't be able to complete it without catching yourself thinking and latching onto something in this way. But when you do, just release it. I like to visualise my thoughts at such times as white doves and I simply release them to fly away.

***

Final Words

This book has been intended as a gentle introduction to mindfulness for those who would normally find it challenging to meditate for even short periods. It is for those whose heads are constantly filled with thoughts of past guilt, regret, negative experiences, or fearful concerns about various aspects of the future.

If you have followed the chapters one by one, with breaks between for practice as suggested, you have probably by now started to notice the benefits of keeping your mind and your body together in the moment.

If you now feel you would like to learn more, there are many excellent books and CDs available as well as locally run courses which will take you to the next level.

If you like things just where you are then that's fine too.

Answers to Test Yourself Questions

3 - DO YOU KNOW WHAT THE BIGGEST HURDLE IS?

1. Which one thing is responsible for most of the negativity we all experience from time to time?

Answer: Our thoughts

2. What is a 'head conversation'?

Answer: When we argue with ourselves in our thoughts, for example, if we think, 'I'd really like that chocolate biscuit .. but I can't I'm on a diet . . . But just one wouldn't hurt surely . . . etc."

3. Before we can begin to change any bad habits what do we need to develop?

Answer: Awareness. Until we become consciously aware of our bad habits and notice when we do them, we can't do anything about changing them.

4 - HOW TO DEVELOP YOUR AWARENESS

1. There are three parts to mindfulness. Which is the first?

Answer: Awareness

2. What does it mean to be 'in the moment'?

Answer: To have your mind on whatever you are experiencing here and now. Not doing one thing whilst your mind is somewhere else.

3. Who or what are naturally good at being 'in the moment'?

Answer: Very young children or pets, because they haven't learnt to talk and so can't use words to think of things other than what they're doing. So whatever they are doing in the here and now usually commands their full attention.

6 - DOES YOUR ALARM SYSTEM NEED A SERVICE?

1. What does the alarm system regard as dangerous?

Answer: Anything which has caused us pain, distress, fear or unhappiness in the past, or anything which we have never come across before and which the alarm system doesn't know about.

2. What happens if you don't respond with a negative feeling (fear, anxiety, sadness) when the alarm system warns you about something?

Answer: The alarm system concludes that it was a mistake to warn you so it stops regarding whatever it was as potentially dangerous and probably won't bring it to your attention again.

8 - STOP THE NEGATIVE PAST COLOURING NOW

1. Through what do we experience our present?

Answer: through the filter of our past experience

2. When you encounter something totally new, what determines whether it's filed as dangerous?

Answer: Your reaction to the warning your alarm system gives you about it. If you react to the warning with anxiety or fear, it gets filed as dangerous. If you react by remaining calm, the alarm system records it as something not to worry about.

9 - WHAT TO DO WHEN YOU CAN'T DO ANYTHING

1. What is the one and only thing which any one of us truly has the power to control?

Answer: Ourselves

2. What is resistance?

Answer: Refusing to accept something which we don't have the power to change.

3. By what means can we change the way we feel about things which have happened to us?

Answer: By changing the way we think about what has happened, by choosing to focus on the neutral or the positive aspects of the situation rather than simply focusing on the negative aspects.

11 - DO WE ALWAYS NEED TO HAVE AN OPINION?

1. What is judgment?

Answer: When we label something as good, bad, pretty, ugly, etc. that is when we classify something according to our beliefs about it. By not passing a judgment on something we are effectively accepting it as it is.

2. When is judgment valid?

Answer: when we have to make a decision about something. For example, if you were in a furniture store buying chairs for your home, it would be valid to pass judgment as to how comfortable the ones in the shop were.

15 - A DIRTY WORD YOU MAY NOT KNOW

Answer: There are things you <u>want</u> to do, there are things you <u>have</u> to do, but there are no things you <u>should</u> do.

End Note

If you have any queries about this book or its contents please go to <u>www.anxaid.com/contact.html</u> and complete the online form.

Other Books by Sue Breton

At the time of publishing this there are two other titles available as either print or ebooks:

"Panic Attacks: A Practical Guide to Recognising and Dealing With Feelings of Panic" This edition published by Vermilion May 2012. First edition published by Martin Dunitz January 1986

"The Blackmailer in Your Head: What To Do About Obsessive Compulsive Disorder" Print edition by Createspace July 2014

More information about these and other titles can be found at

www.anxaid.com/publications.html

Link to Meditation Downloads

All these meditation tracks are in mp3 format and can be downloaded by Right-Click (Ctrl-Click on Mac) on the relevant button shown on webpage

www.anxaid.com/cwmmp3.html

The download page is password-protected.

The password is c1w2dTt (case sensitive)

Meditation Instructions

PLEASE NOTE

These instructions are for those who are unable to download and listen to the introductory meditation tracks for any reason. Each of these is easier done by listening at least initially although it is still possible to learn the basics from written instructions provided these are followed.

1. BRIEF TOUCH MEDITATION

This meditation involves placing your awareness on the sensation of touch. Place you hand, palm down, on whatever is nearby. Then, as you move your palm to and fro, observe the sensations you can feel.

If, for example, you are touching fabric you may notice that the sensations change when you change direction.

As you do this you may notice your mind wander off or you may catch yourself describing what you are feeling in words. If this happens simply move your focus back to the sensations alone.

This meditation can be done for only 20-30 seconds at a time if need be. Keeping the head and body focused together without thoughts even for such a short time is beneficial.

2. MEDITATING ON SOUND

The easiest way to meditate on sound is to imagine your head is a microphone. Like a microphone, your ears pick up random sounds from different directions. These may be sounds from in the room, from outside, or even from your own body. You are aware of sound but you don't have to think about it or try and work out what's making it.

You will find that your brain tries to be helpful and tells you or gives you images about what it thinks is responsible for the sound, but you don't engage with any of this. Simply allow sound to register and pass on by.

3. MEDITATING ON BREATH

This is a simple meditation that can be done anywhere at any time. Breath is always there and we don't have to focus on it in order for it to keep going. So, because breathing will just keep happening, all we have to do is observe it.

Start by allowing yourself to notice any sensations in your nostrils or throat as the air enters your body. Follow the breath and observe which part of your body moves with each breath. You don't try and make anything in particular move, you simply observe what happens anyway.

As the breath leaves your body you are still with it, observing any sensations of the air passing out, however slight these may be.

Between one breath and the next there will be a slight pause—just be aware of this but don't try to control it.

Any time during this exercise that you catch yourself thinking or your mind wanders off, just place it back onto an awareness of your breath again and carry on.

Don't be surprised if you can barely maintain awareness of your breath for more than a single breath at a time at first. The exercise is about noticing when your mind has wandered and leading it back again. Practising by focusing on just a single breath or two at odd times during the day will help develop the skill.

4. MEDITATING ON TWINGES

This meditation is an introduction to using mindfulness to manage negative emotions such as frustration or pain. Before you can hope to use this for something that is really troublesome, you will need to practise the technique on minor discomforts or irritations.

The audio track uses the suggestion of having an itch on your nose or face. This will work if it suggested by someone else but it is not so easy to imagine an itch for yourself. Therefore you will have to grab a chance to practise this in everyday life by watching out for any minor discomfort such as pins and needles, or needing to shift body position while sitting, or maybe even a minor insect bite.

When you become aware of such a discomfort you allow your awareness to focus on it but you do so without wishing it would go away. You do not resist the sensation of whatever it is but you observe it for its own sake. You notice the area it covers and the nature of the sensation it is causing. Then you direct each breath to it in your mind as you breathe. Usually this causes the discomfort to either move elsewhere where it seems not to bother you so much, or it may even disappear.

5. LETTING GO OF THOUGHTS MEDITATION

Before doing this meditation you have to choose the imagery you will use. This includes what you will write the thought on to allow it to pass by. This was described in Chapter 17. You then carry out a meditation on breath or sound, but whenever you become aware that you are thinking, you imagine writing the thought, letter by letter, onto your chosen image, then watch it carried by, and return to the meditation.

If you do this with thoughts that don't really matter, you develop the skill. In addition your brain learns to associate the image you have chosen with dropping what it was thinking. Once this link is well-established through practice, you can simply imagine your scene whenever you are troubled by a particular thought, see it carried away, and your brain will be willing to let it go. In order for this to work effectively, however, you will need to train your brain by practising.

6. AWARENESS OF WHAT COMES AND GOES

This simply means that you allow yourself to be aware of whatever sensations are passing through. These may be sounds, smells, sensations of touch, thoughts, etc. Whatever your mind finds, you acknowledge it is there and simply move beyond it. It is what you did as a small child before you learnt language.

You are aware you are living in your surroundings, you are receiving input from your surroundings, but you are not thinking about anything on purpose. Thoughts may enter your mind but you notice these as if they are simply comments made by a voice on the radio. You don't engage with them and think about them. You just let them go by.

***

Printed in Great Britain
by Amazon.co.uk, Ltd.,
Marston Gate.